FOR ORGANS, PIANOS & ELECTRONIC KEYBOARDS

E-Z PLAY TODAY
217

MOVIE BALLADS

2nd Edition

ISBN 978-0-7935-7926-6

HAL•LEONARD®
CORPORATION
7777 W. BLUEMOUND RD. P.O. BOX 13819 MILWAUKEE, WI 53213

Visit Hal Leonard Online at
www.halleonard.com

MOVIE

CONTENTS

BALLADS

Alfie
Theme from the Paramount Picture ALFIE

Registration 9
Rhythm: 8-Beat or Pops

Words by Hal David
Music by Burt Bacharach

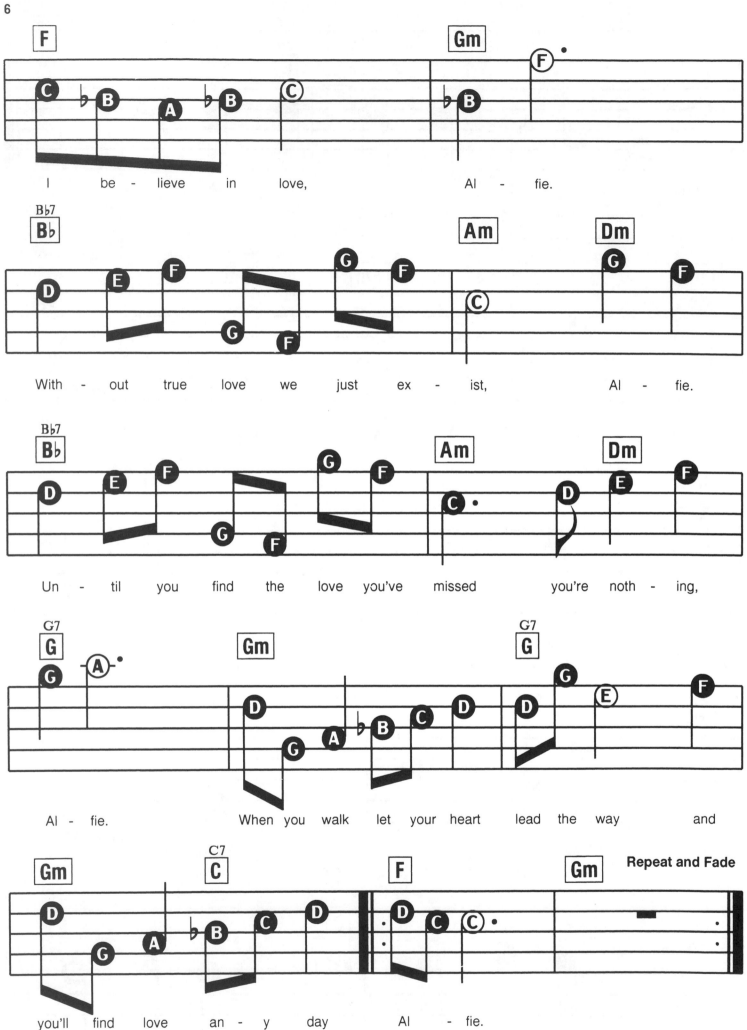

Can You Feel the Love Tonight
from Walt Disney Pictures' THE LION KING

Registration 1
Rhythm: Ballad or Pops

Music by Elton John
Lyrics by Tim Rice

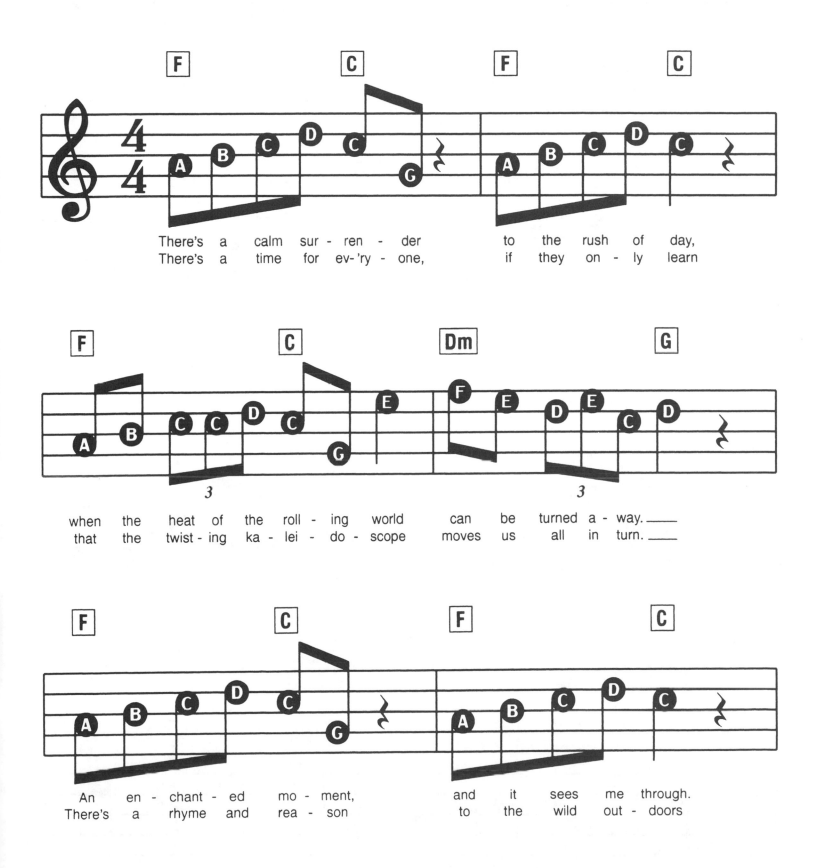

There's a   calm   sur - ren - der   to   the   rush   of   day,
There's a   time   for   ev-'ry - one,   if   they   on - ly   learn

when   the   heat   of   the   roll - ing   world   can   be   turned   a - way. ____
that   the   twist - ing   ka - lei - do - scope   moves   us   all   in   turn. ____

An   en - chant - ed   mo - ment,   and   it   sees   me   through.
There's a   rhyme   and   rea - son   to   the   wild   out - doors

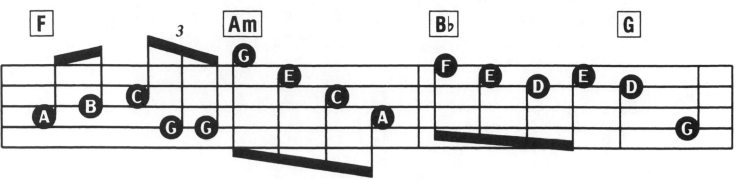

It's e - nough for this rest - less war - rior just to be with you.
when the heart of this star - crossed voy - ag - er beats in time with yours. } And

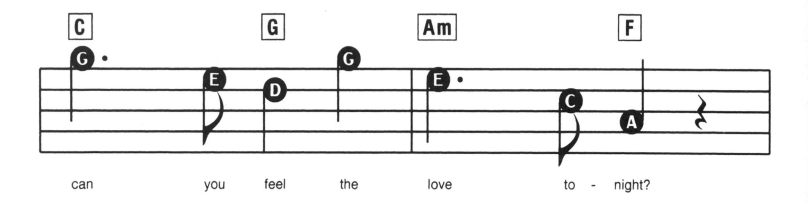

can you feel the love to - night?

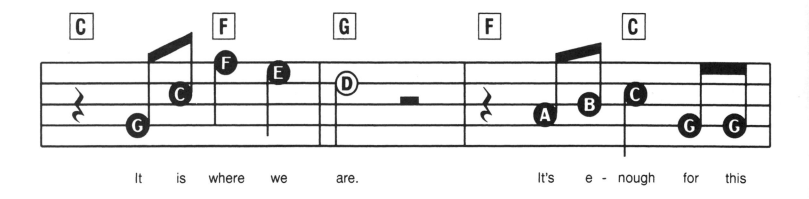

It is where we are. It's e - nough for this

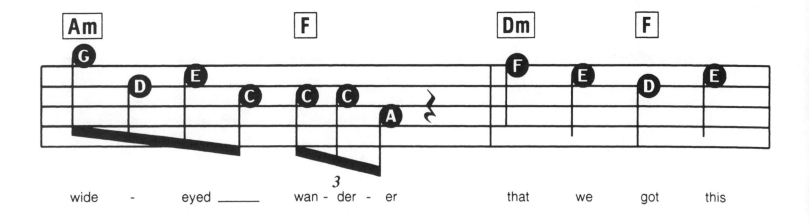

wide - eyed _____ wan - der - er that we got this

Arrivederci, Roma
(Goodbye to Rome)
from the Motion Picture SEVEN HILLS OF ROME

Registration 3
Rhythm: Latin

Words and Music by Carl Sigman, Ranucci Renato,
Sandro Giovanni and Peidro Garinei

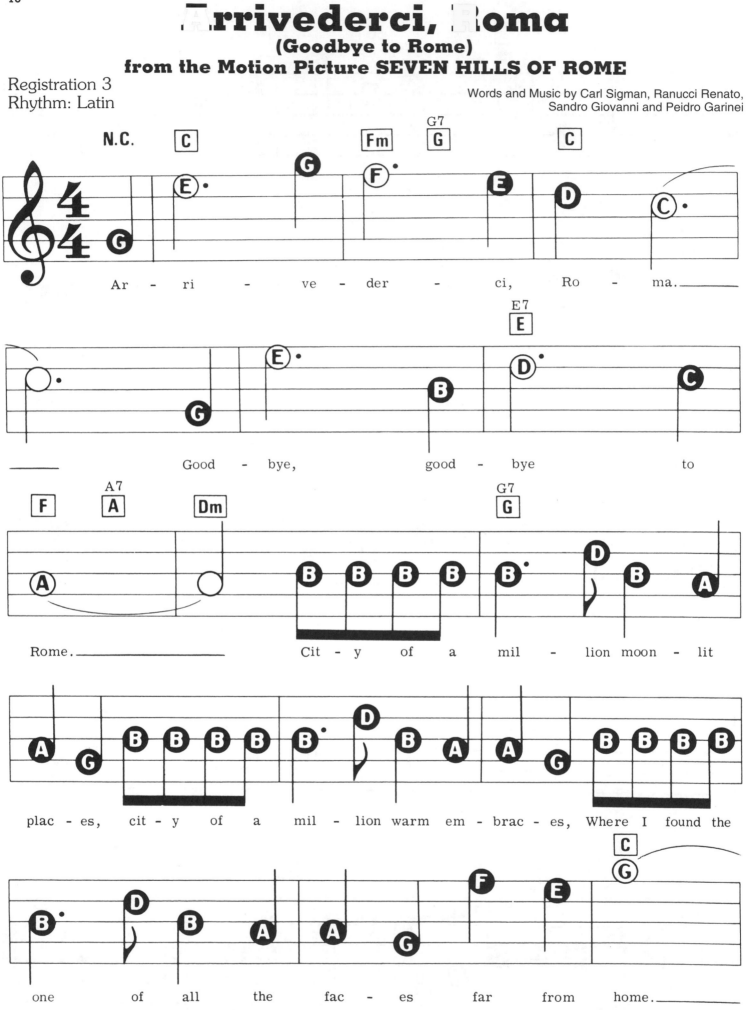

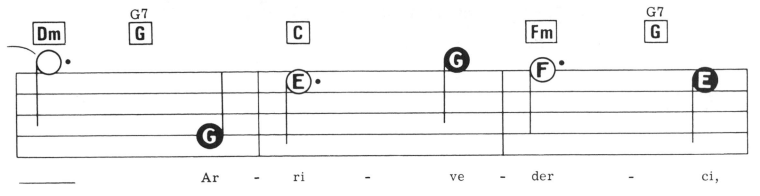

Ar - ri - ve - der - ci,

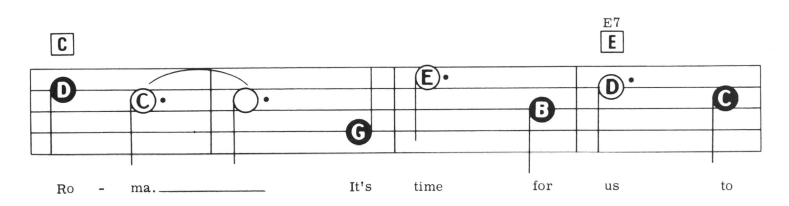

Ro - ma._____ It's time for us to

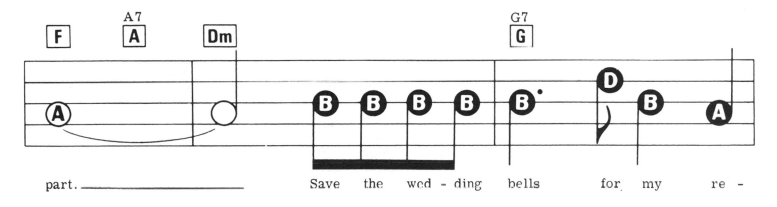

part._____ Save the wed - ding bells for my re -

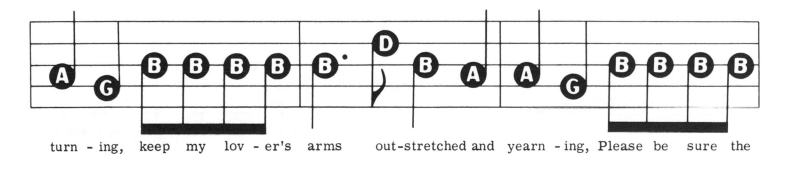

turn - ing, keep my lov - er's arms out-stretched and yearn - ing, Please be sure the

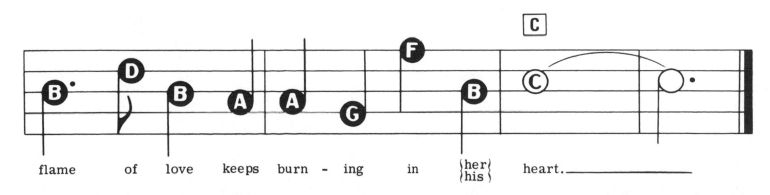

flame of love keeps burn - ing in {her}{his} heart._____

Beauty and the Beast

from Walt Disney's BEAUTY AND THE BEAST

Registration 1
Rhythm: Pops or 8-Beat

Lyrics by Howard Ashman
Music by Alan Menken

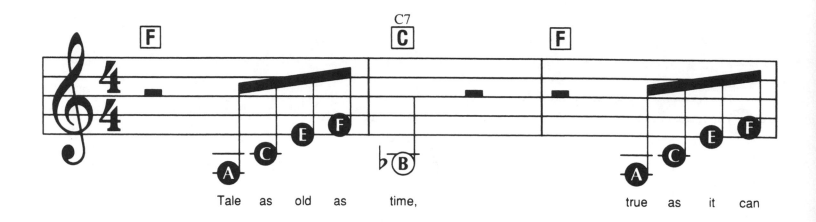

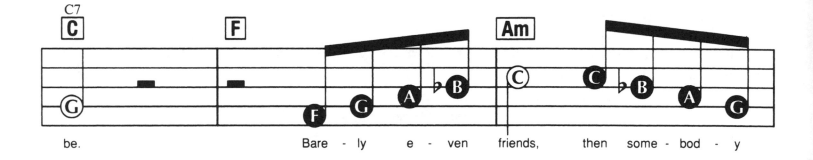

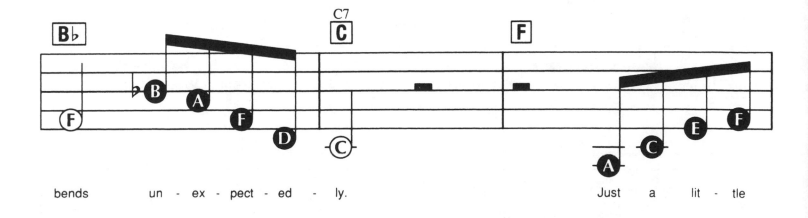

13

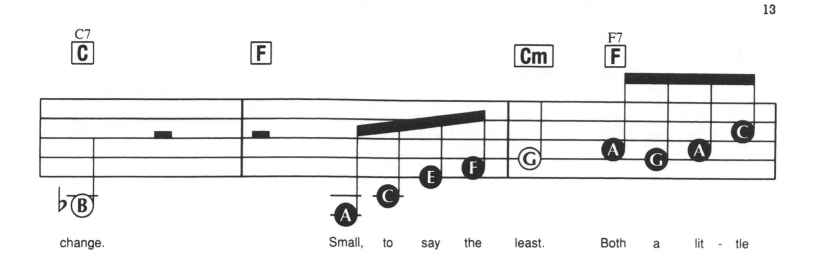

change.　　　　　Small, to say the least. Both a lit - tle

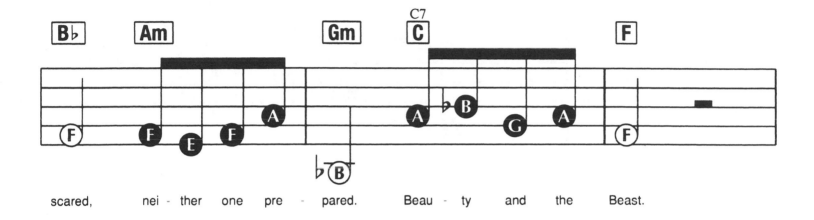

scared, nei - ther one pre - pared. Beau - ty and the Beast.

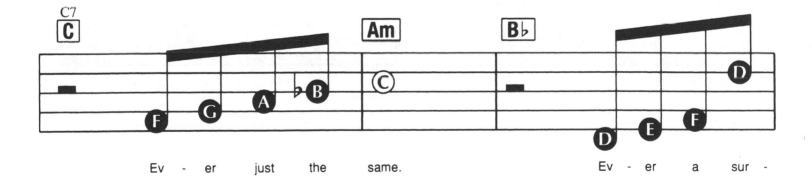

Ev - er just the same.　　　　Ev - er a sur -

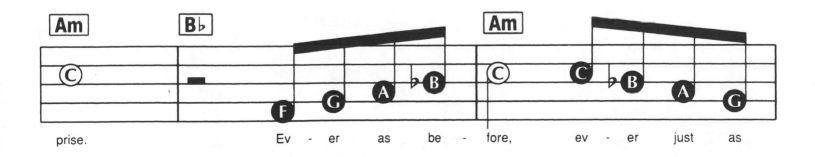

prise.　　　　Ev - er as be - fore, ev - er just as

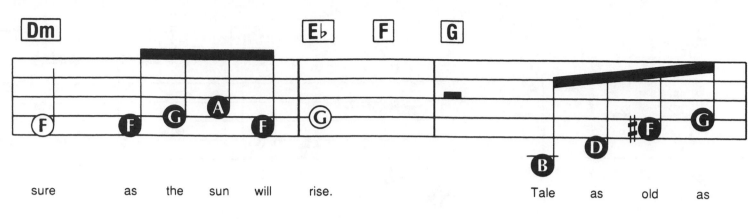

sure   as   the   sun   will   rise.   Tale   as   old   as

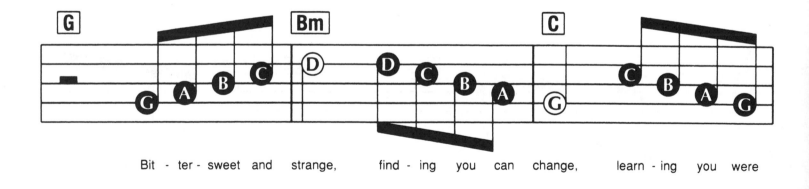

time.   Tune   as   old   as   song.

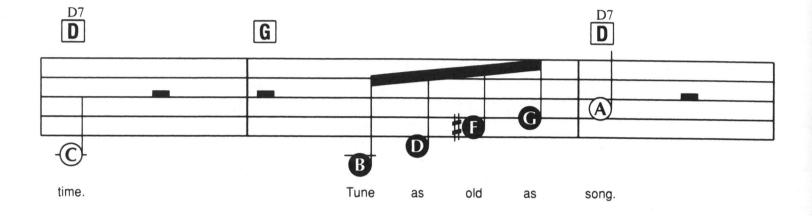

Bit - ter - sweet and   strange,   find - ing   you   can   change,   learn - ing   you   were

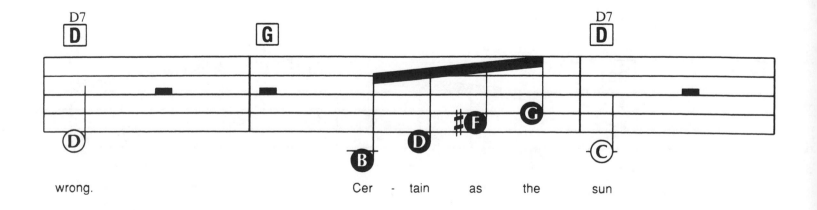

wrong.   Cer - tain   as   the   sun

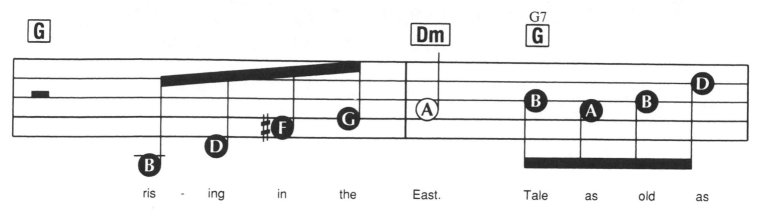

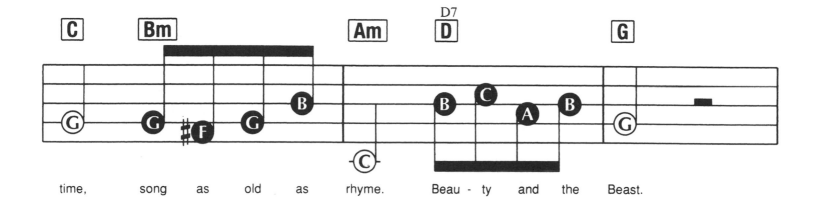

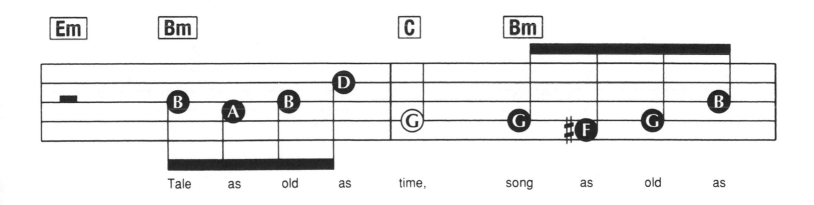

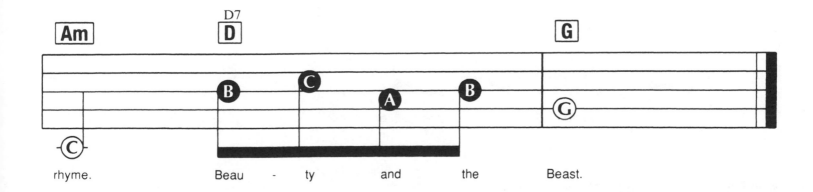

Bless the Beasts and Children
from BLESS THE BEASTS AND CHILDREN

Registration 3
Rhythm: Slow Rock or Ballad

Words and Music by Barry DeVorzon
and Perry Botkin, Jr.

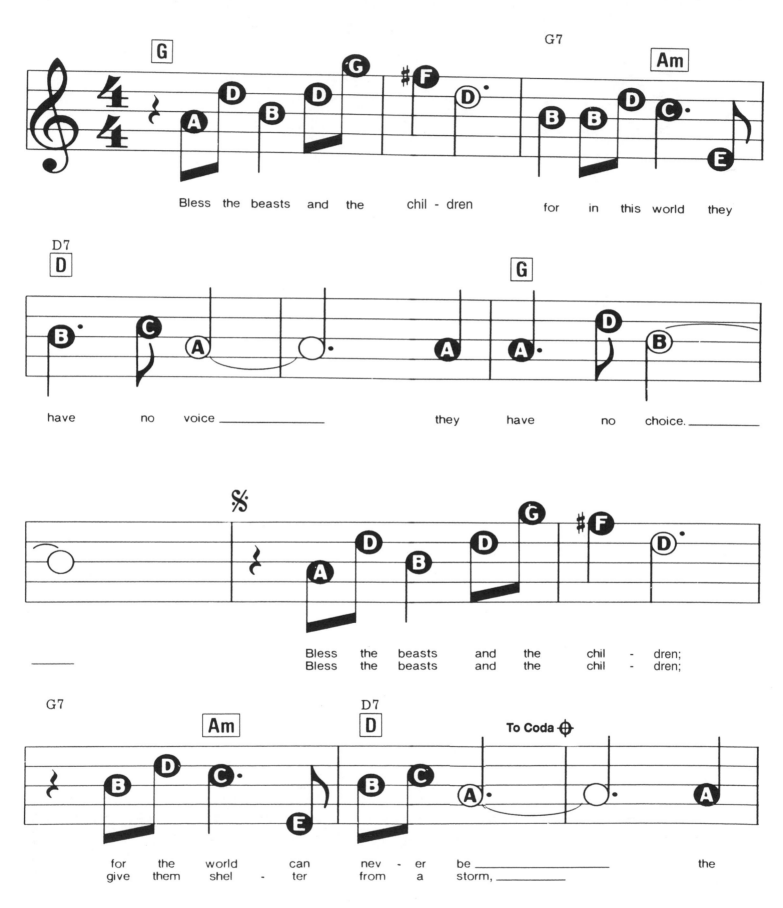

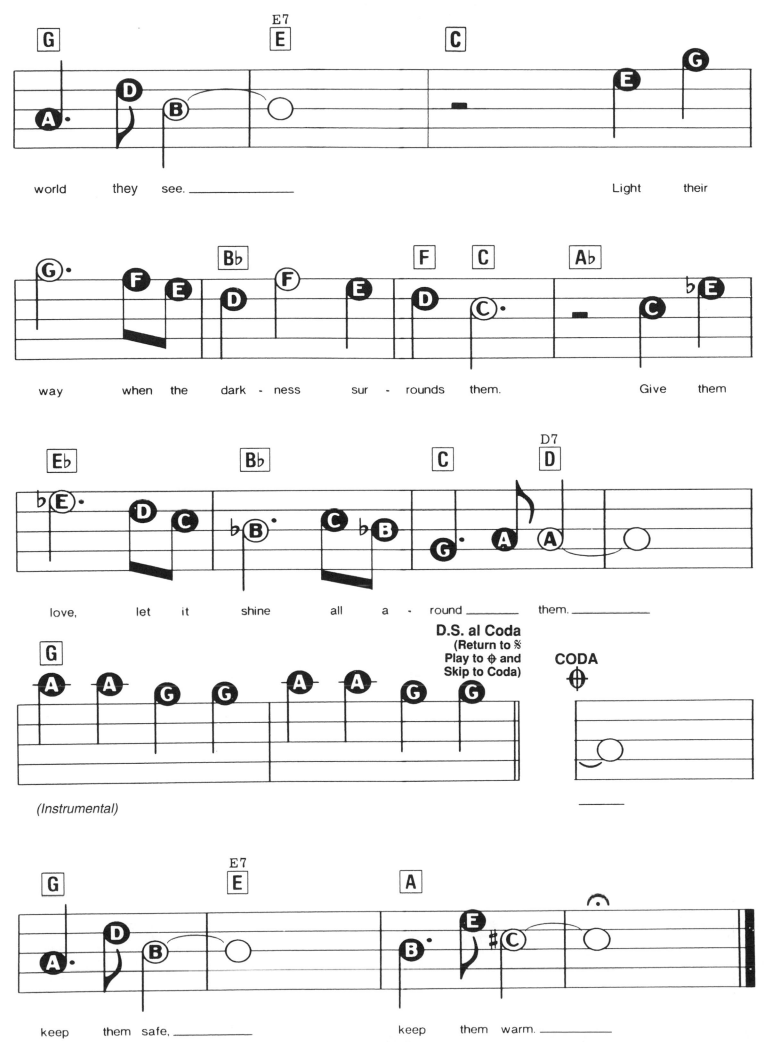

Born Free
from the Columbia Pictures' Release BORN FREE

Registration 4
Rhythm: Ballad or Slow Rock

Words by Don Black
Music by John Barry

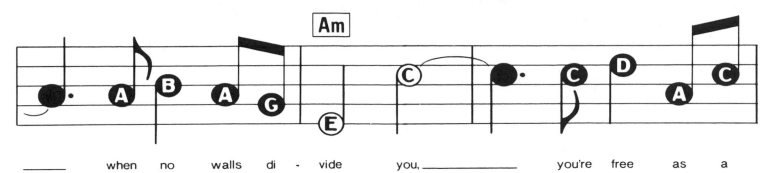

_____ when no walls di - vide you, _____ you're free as a

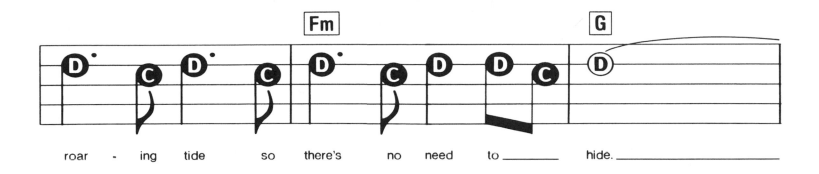

roar - ing tide so there's no need to _____ hide. _____

G7

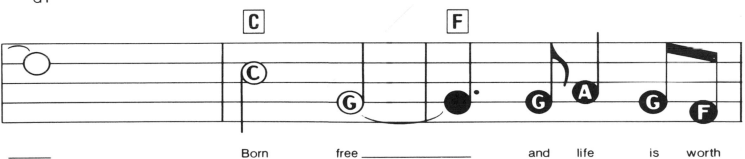

_____ Born free _____ and life is worth

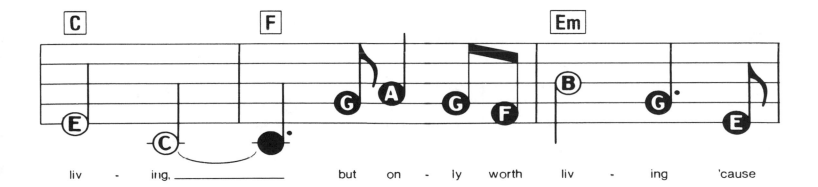

liv - ing, _____ but on - ly worth liv - ing 'cause

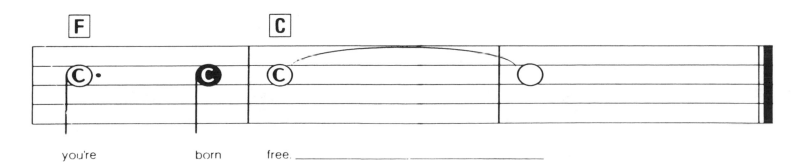

you're born free. _____

Call Me Irresponsible

from the Paramount Picture PAPA'S DELICATE CONDITION

Registration 8
Rhythm: Swing or Ballad

Words by Sammy Cahn
Music by James Van Heusen

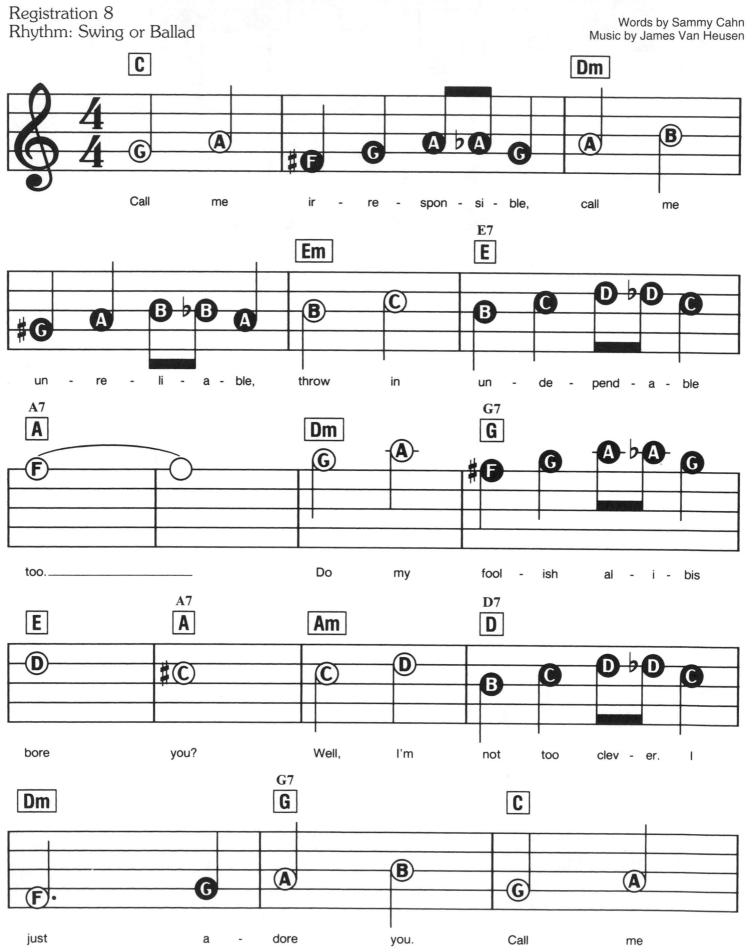

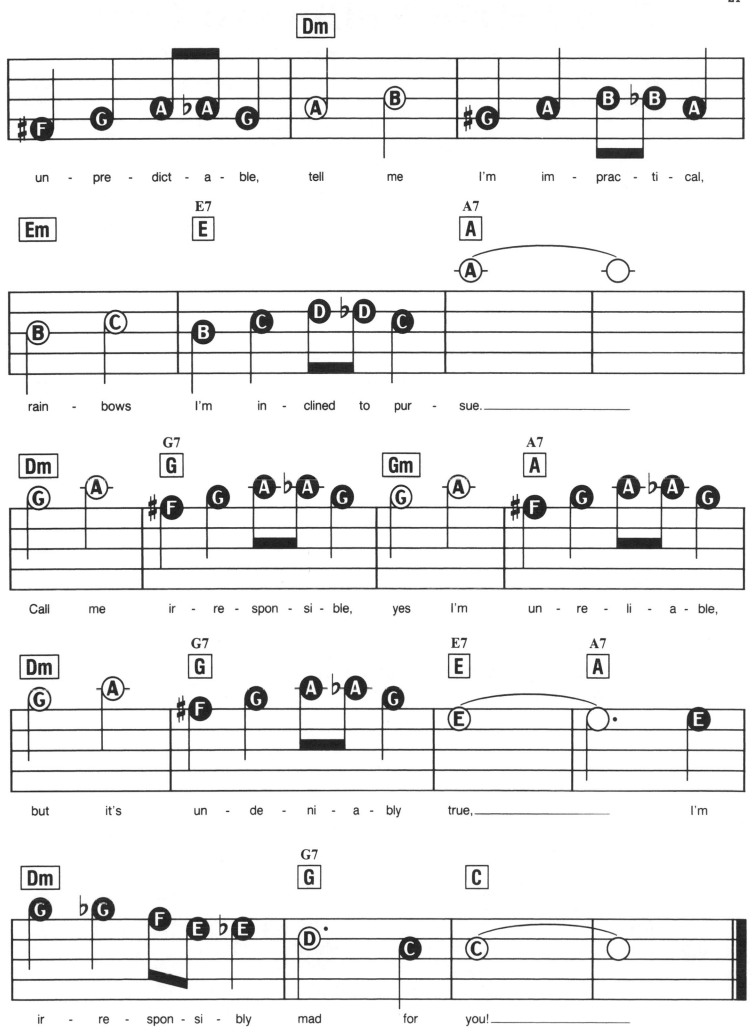

Can't Help Falling in Love

from the Paramount Picture BLUE HAWAII

Registration 3
Rhythm: Ballad or Swing

Words and Music by George David Weiss,
Hugo Peretti and Luigi Creatore

Wise men say on - ly
Shall I stay? Would it

fools rush in, but I can't
be a sin if I can't

help fall - ing in love with you.
help fall - ing in love with you?

Like a riv - er flows sure - ly to the sea,

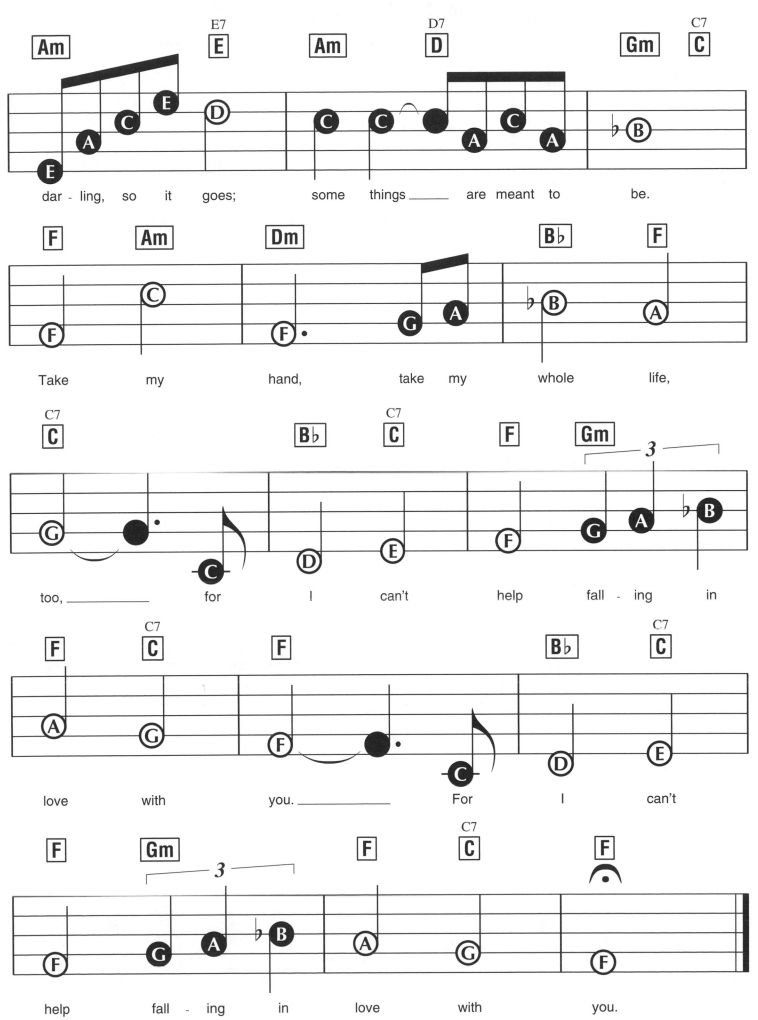

Cheek to Cheek
from the RKO Radio Motion Picture TOP HAT

Registration 1
Rhythm: Fox Trot or Swing

Words and Music by
Irving Berlin

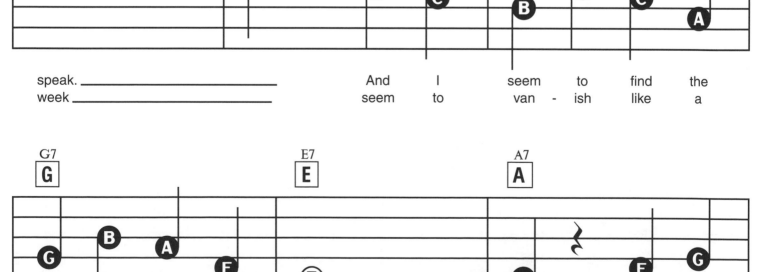

© Copyright 1935 by Irving Berlin
Copyright Renewed
International Copyright Secured All Rights Reserved

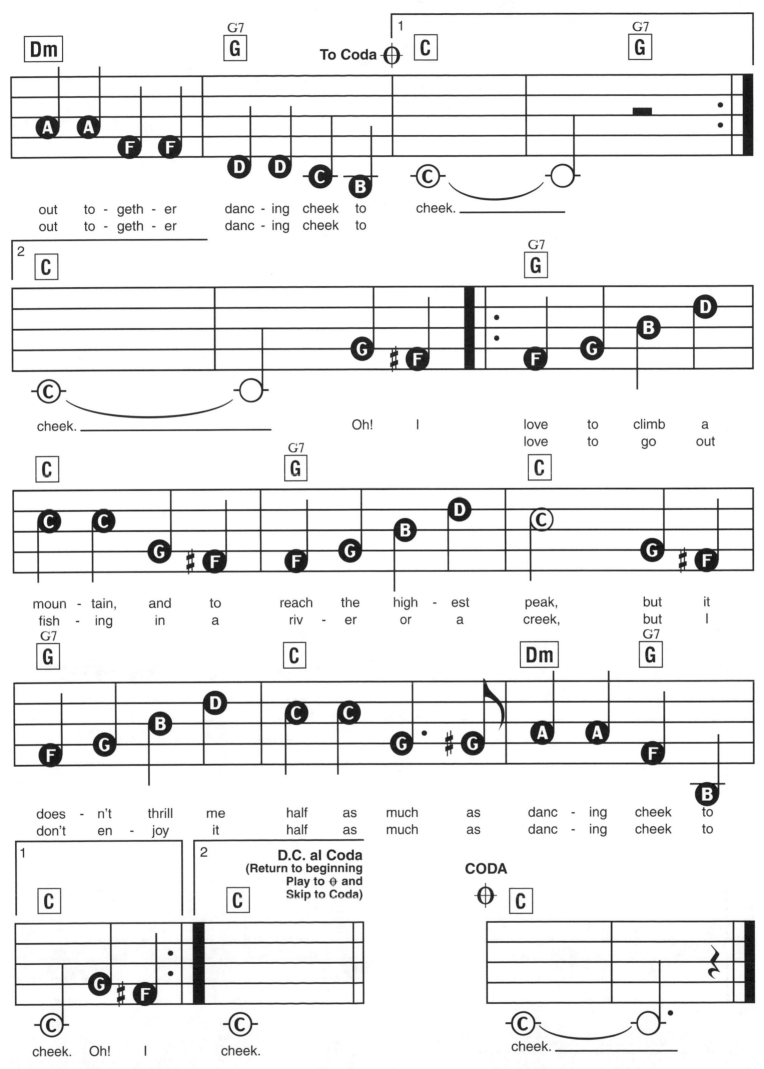

Do You Know Where You're Going To?

Theme from MAHOGANY

Registration 5
Rhythm: Slow Rock or Ballad

Words by Gerry Goffin
Music by Michael Masser

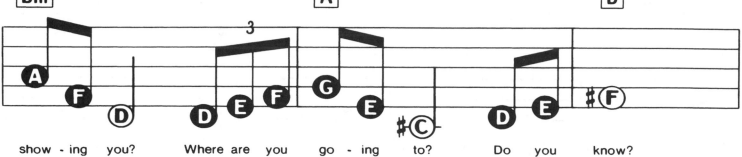

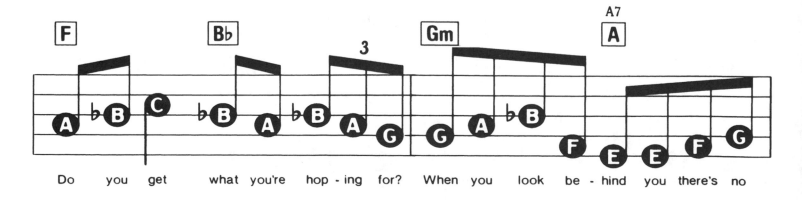

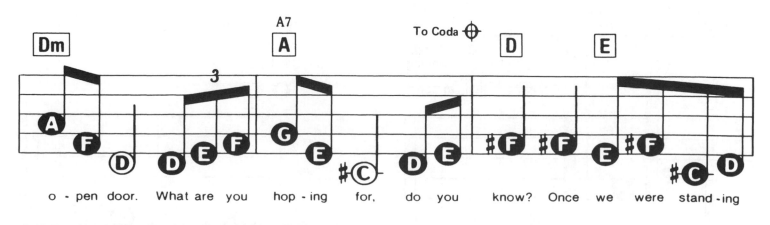

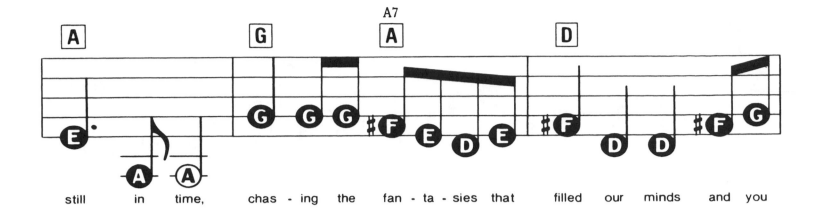

still in time, chas - ing the fan - ta - sies that filled our minds and you

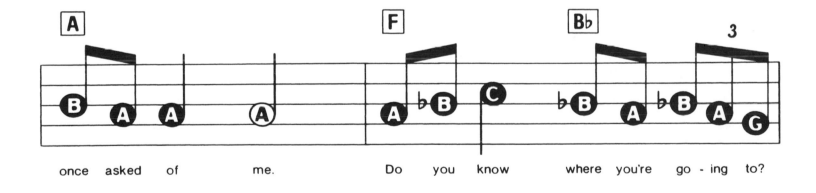

knew how I loved you but my spir - it was free, laugh-ing at the ques -tions that you

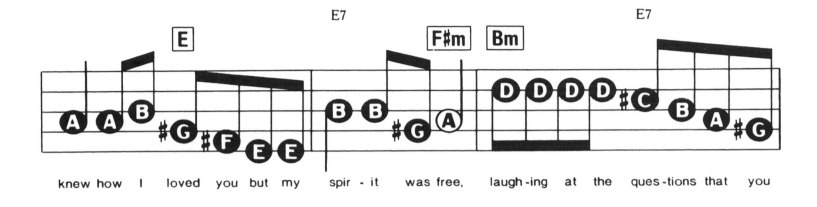

once asked of me. Do you know where you're go - ing to?

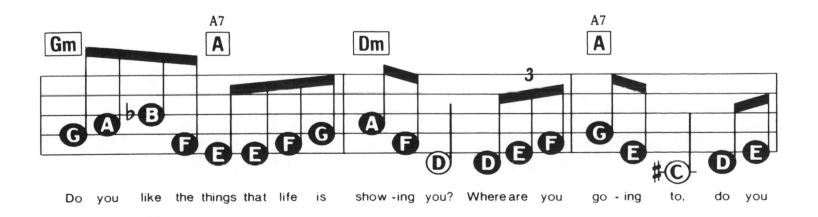

Do you like the things that life is show-ing you? Where are you go - ing to, do you

28

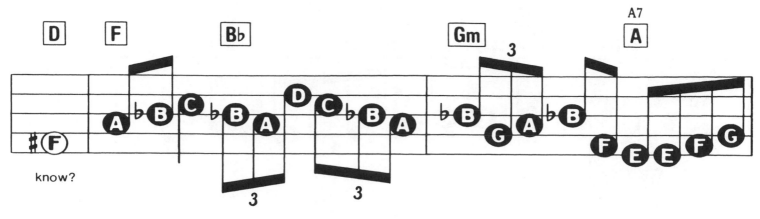

know?

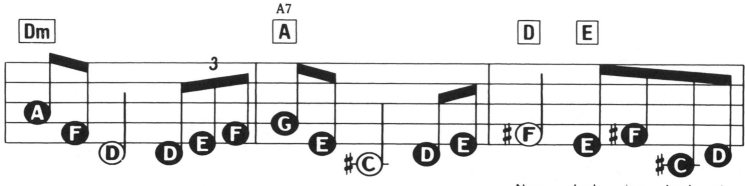

Now look - ing back at

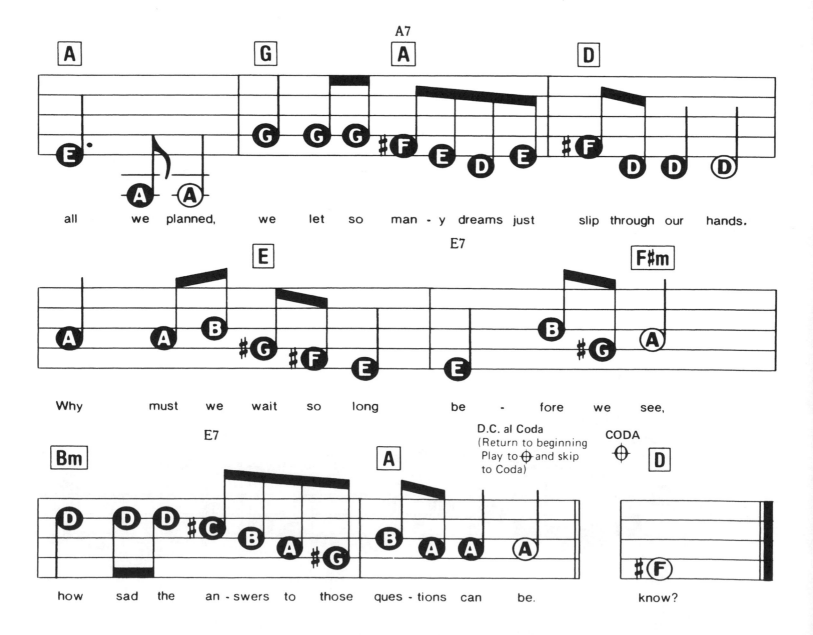

all we planned, we let so man - y dreams just slip through our hands.

Why must we wait so long be - fore we see,

D.C. al Coda
(Return to beginning
Play to ⊕ and skip
to Coda)

CODA ⊕

how sad the an - swers to those ques - tions can be.

know?

The Glory of Love
featured in GUESS WHO'S COMING TO DINNER

Registration 3
Rhythm: Swing or Ballad

Words and Music by
Billy Hill

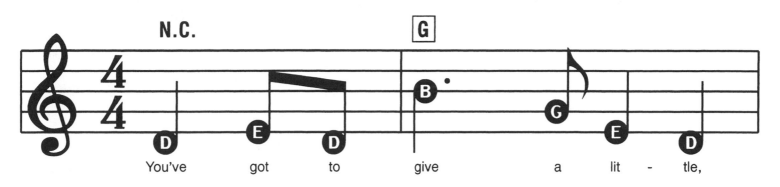

You've got to give a lit - tle,

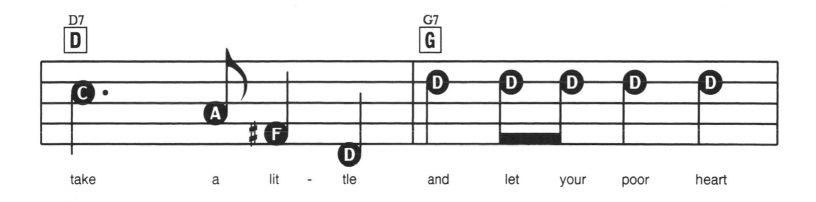

take a lit - tle and let your poor heart

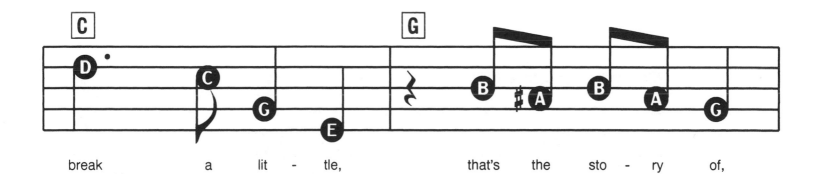

break a lit - tle, that's the sto - ry of,

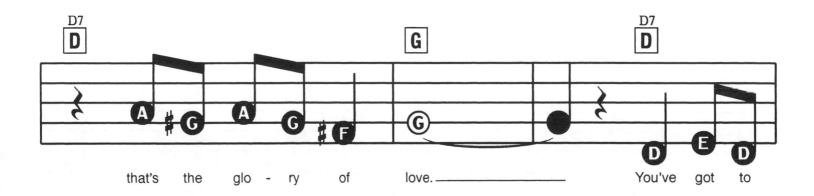

that's the glo - ry of love. _____ You've got to

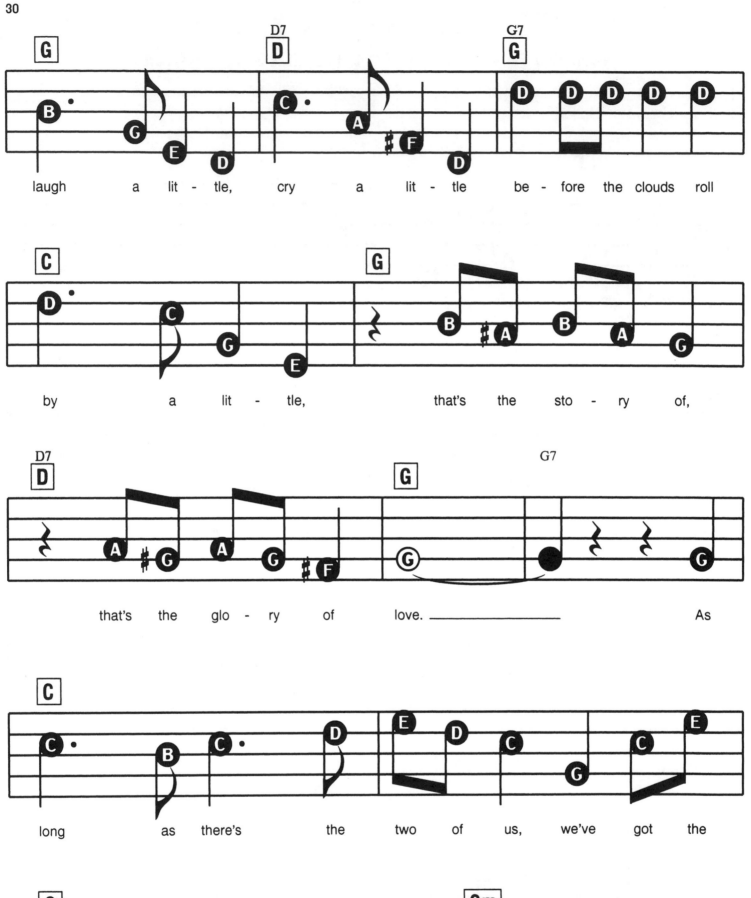
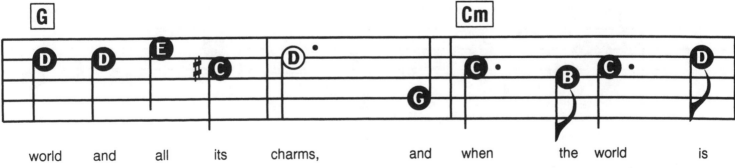

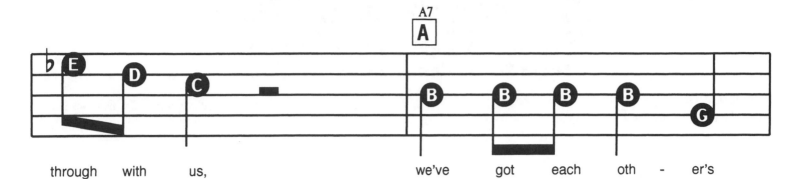

through with us,   we've   got   each   oth - er's

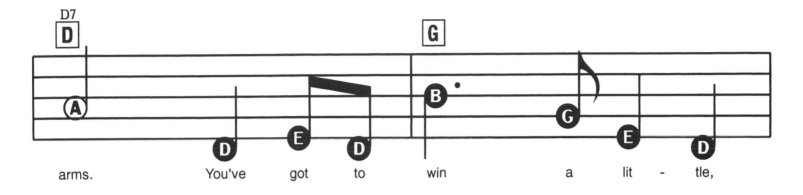

arms.   You've   got   to   win   a   lit - tle,

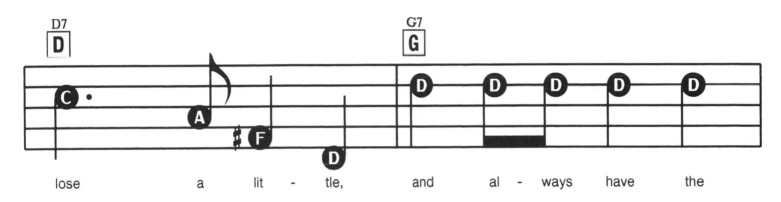

lose   a   lit - tle,   and   al - ways   have   the

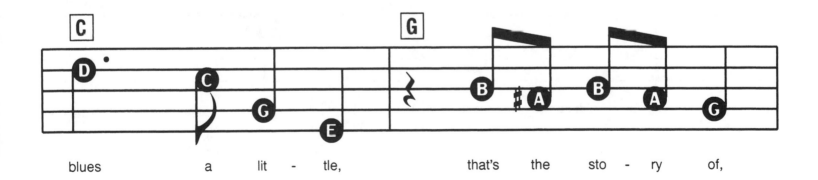

blues   a   lit - tle,   that's   the   sto - ry   of,

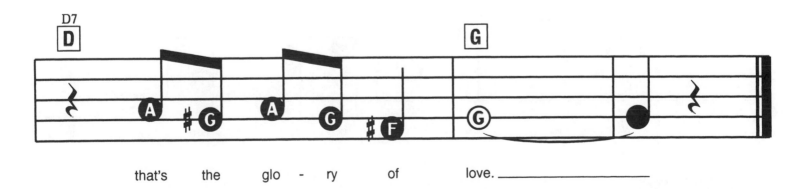

that's   the   glo - ry   of   love. _____

A Dream Is a Wish
Your Heart Makes
from Walt Disney's CINDERELLA

Registration 1
Rhythm: Ballad or Fox Trot

Words and Music by Mack David,
Al Hoffman and Jerry Livingston

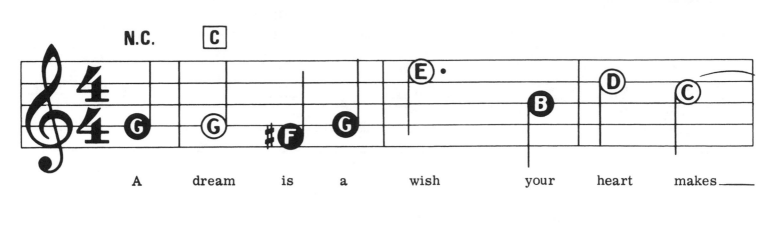

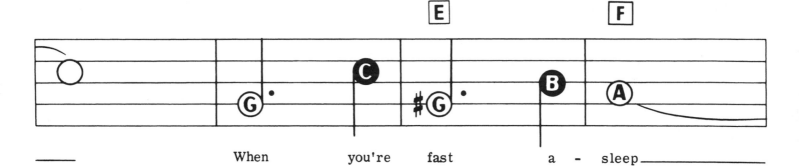

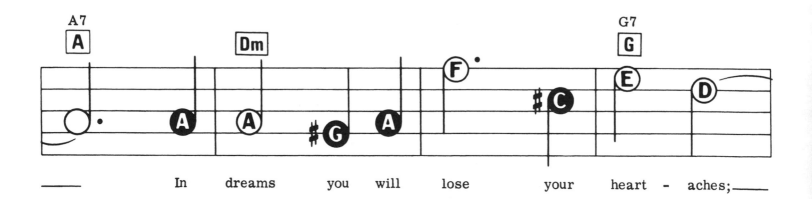

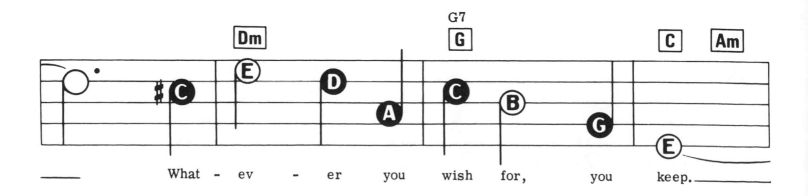

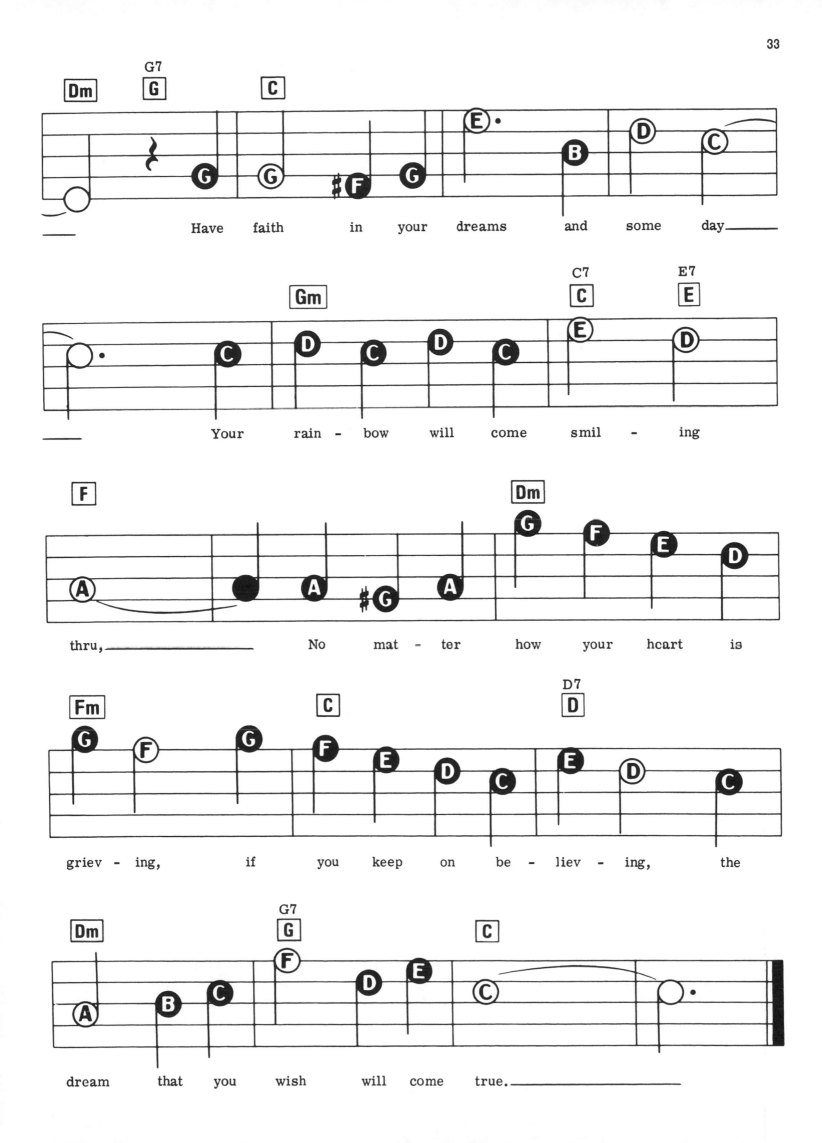

I'm Old Fashioned
from YOU WERE NEVER LOVELIER

Registration 5
Rhythm: Fox Trot or Ballad

Words by Johnny Mercer
Music by Jerome Kern

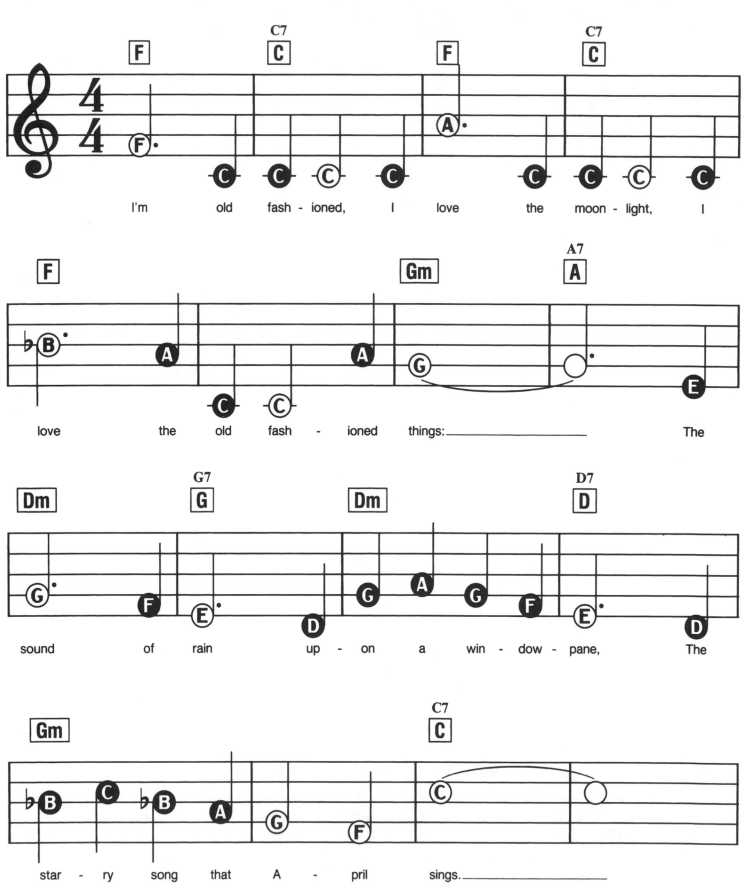

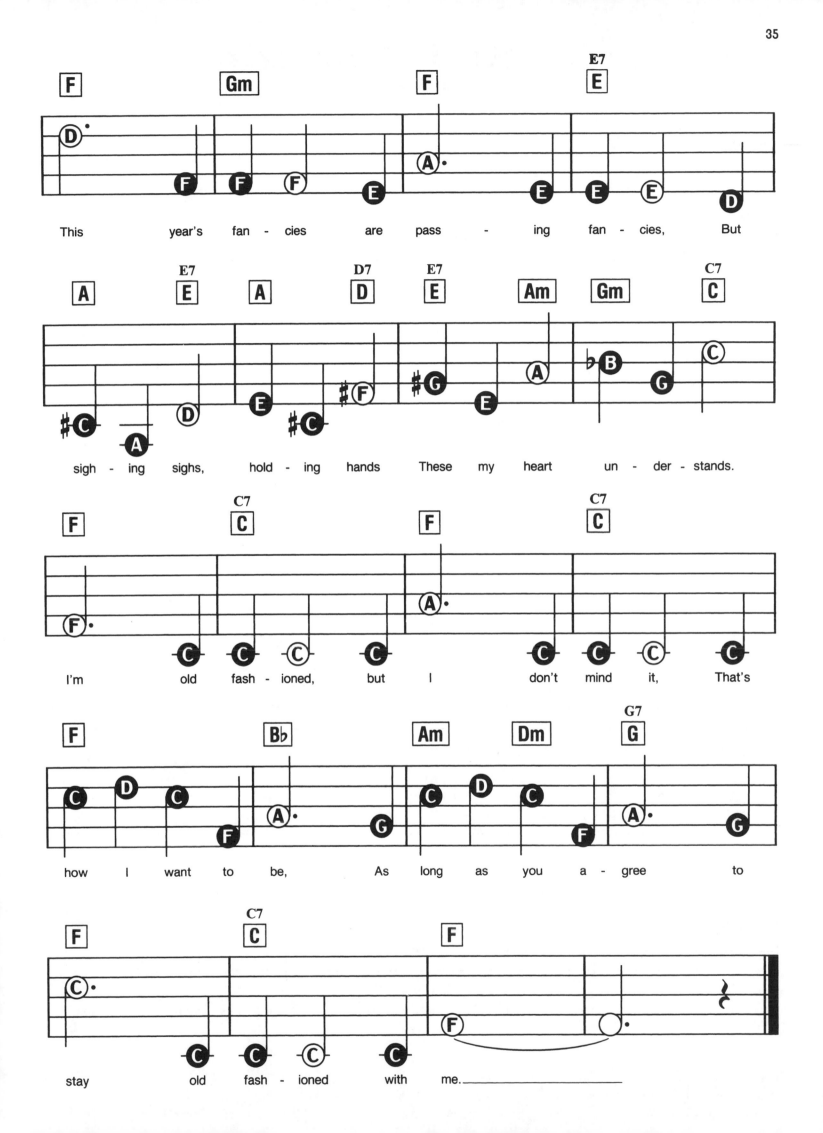

In the Still of the Night
from ROSALIE

Registration 2
Rhythm: Latin

Words and Music by
Cole Porter

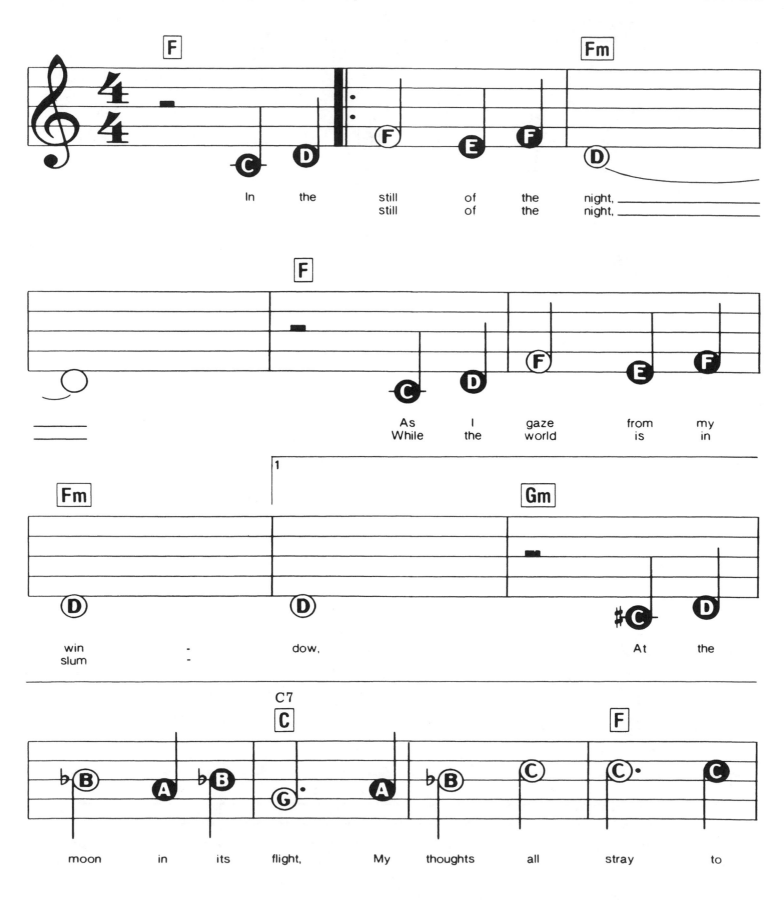

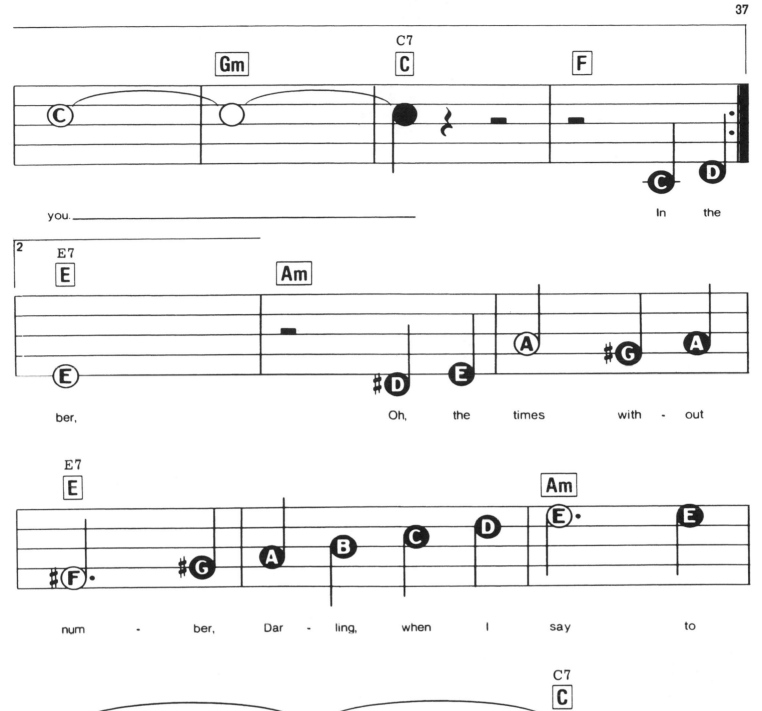

you. _____ In the

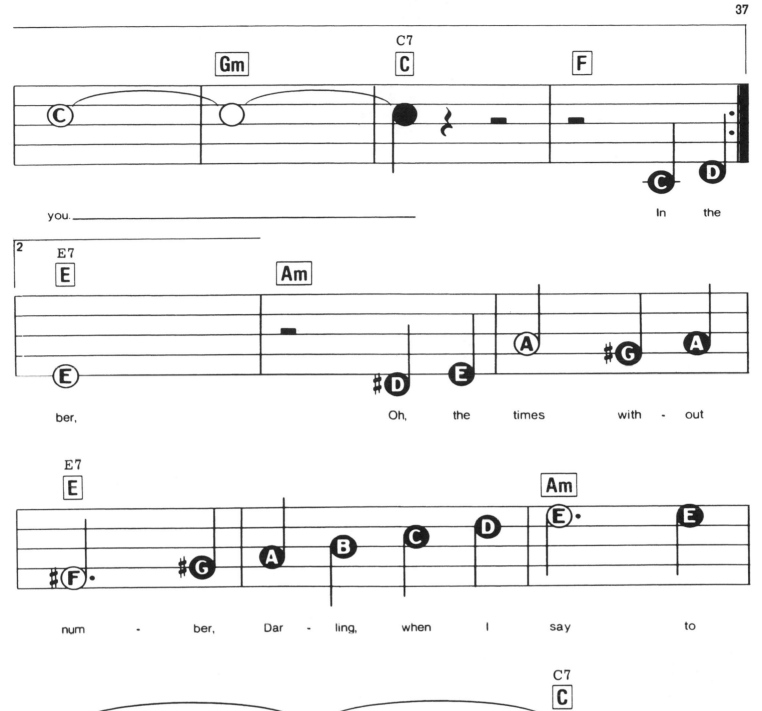

ber, Oh, the times with - out

num - ber, Dar - ling, when I say to

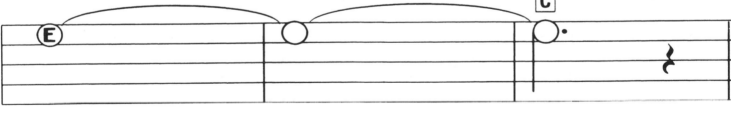

you: _____

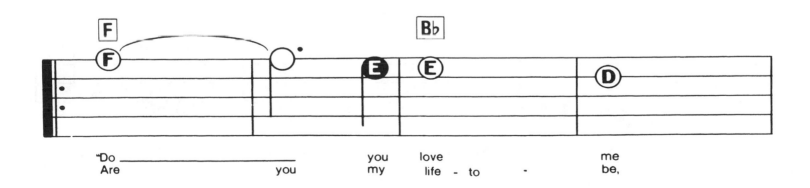

"Do _____ you love me
Are you my life - to - be,

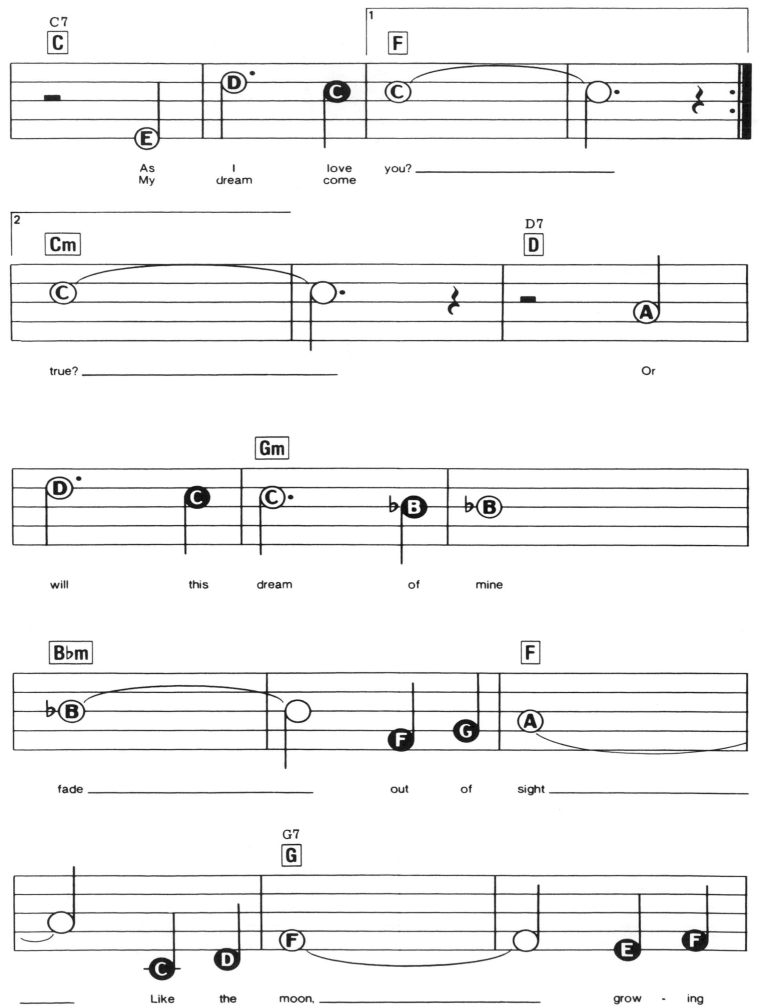

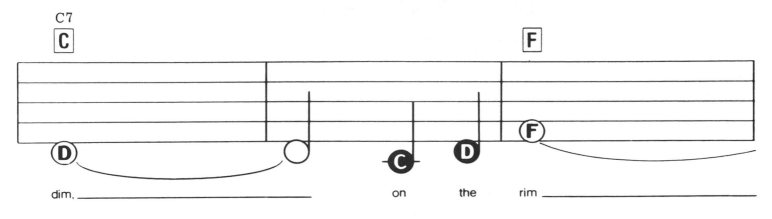

dim, _____ on the rim _____

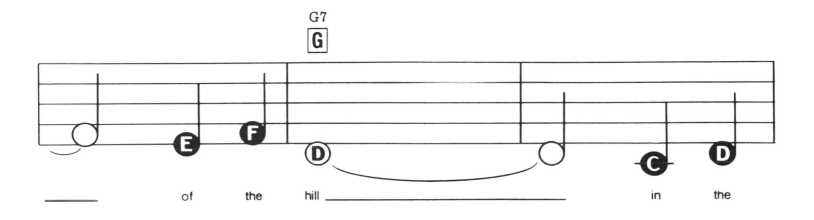

_____ of the hill _____ in the

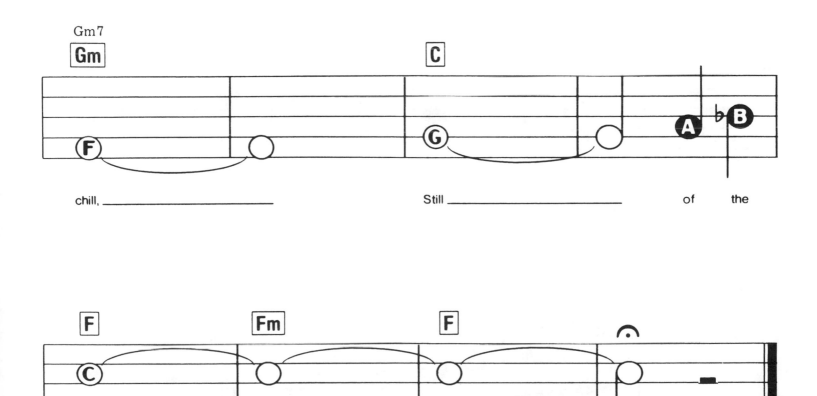

chill, _____ Still _____ of the

night? _____

Isn't It Romantic?
from the Paramount Picture LOVE ME TONIGHT

Registration 2
Rhythm: Swing or Ballad

Words by Lorenz Hart
Music by Richard Rodgers

Is - n't it ro - man - tic? Mu - sic in the night, a
man - tic? Mere - ly to be young on

dream that can be heard. Is - n't it ro - man - tic?
such a night as this? Is - n't it ro - man - tic?

Mov - ing shad - ows write the old - est mag - ic word.
Ev - 'ry note that's sung is like a lov - er's kiss.

I hear the breez - es play - ing in the trees a -
Sweet sym - bols in the moon - light.

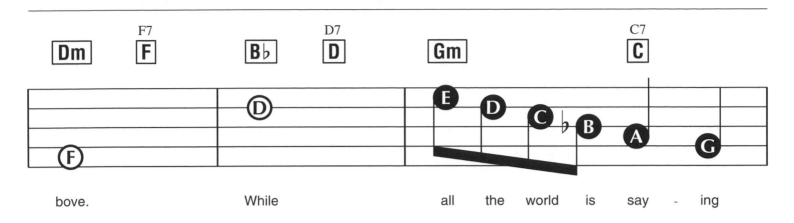

bove.   While   all the world is say - ing

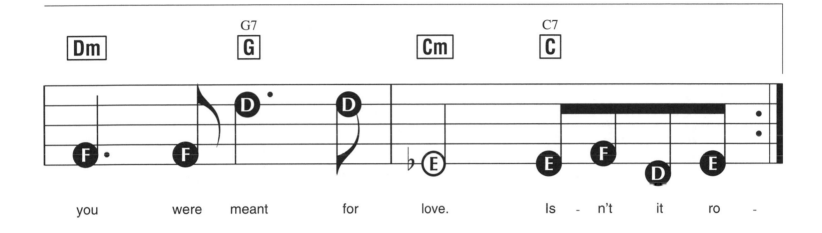

you   were meant   for   love.   Is - n't it ro -

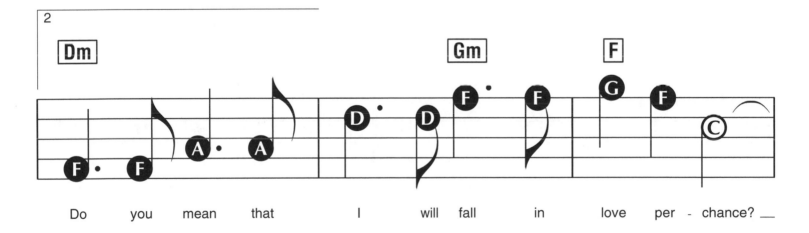

Do   you   mean   that   I   will fall   in   love per - chance? __

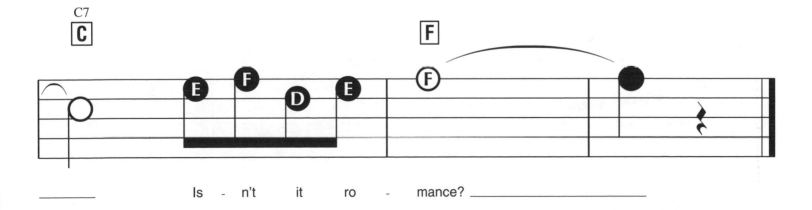

_____   Is - n't it ro - mance? _____

It Might as Well Be Spring
from STATE FAIR

Registration 3
Rhythm: Ballad

Lyrics by Oscar Hammerstein II
Music by Richard Rodgers

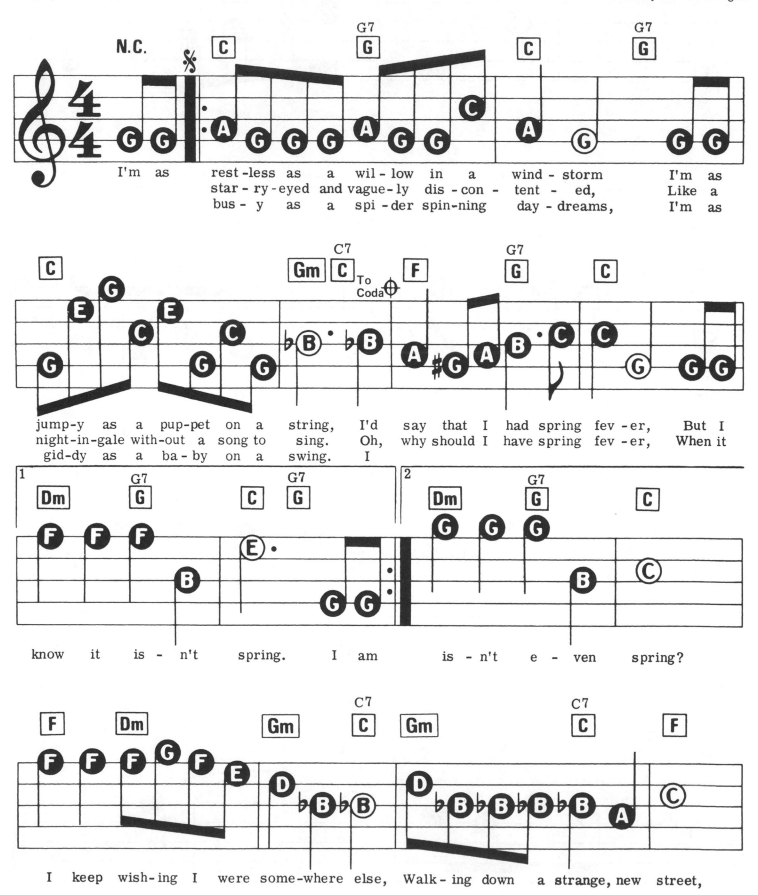

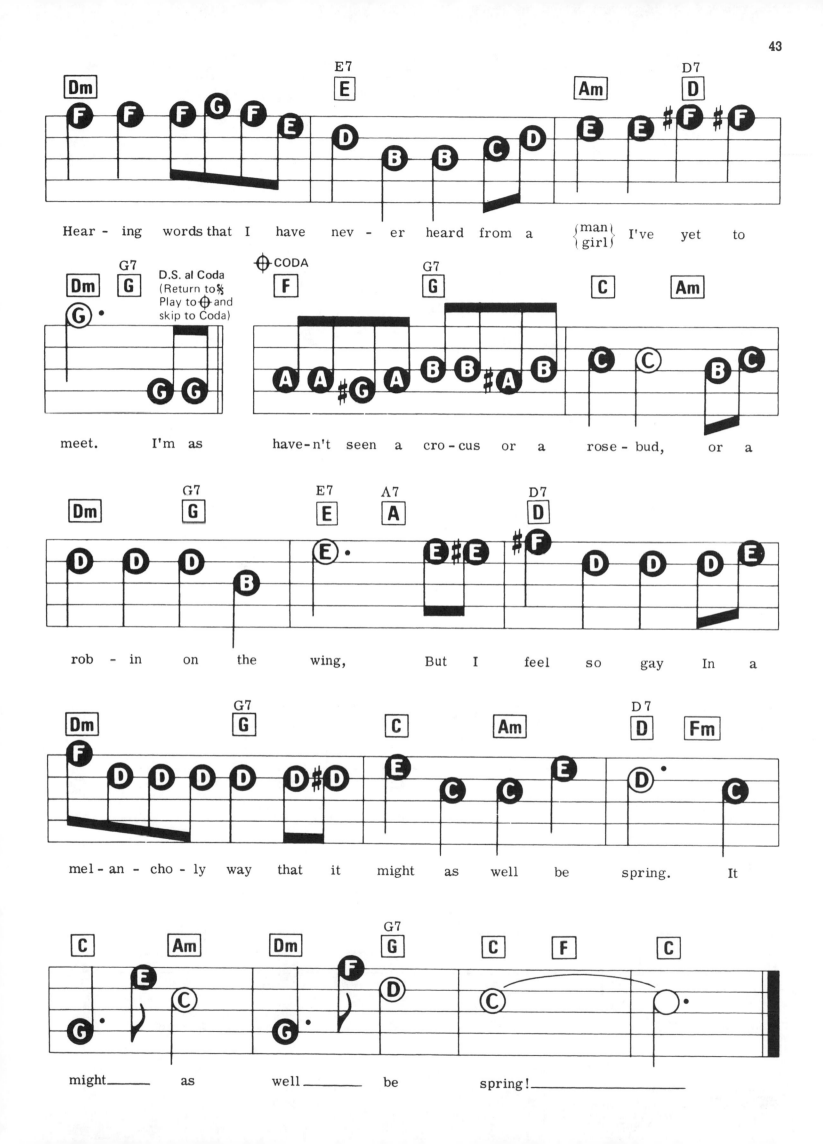

43

Let's Face the Music and Dance
from the Motion Picture FOLLOW THE FLEET

Registration 3
Rhythm: Swing or Ballad

Words and Music by
Irving Berlin

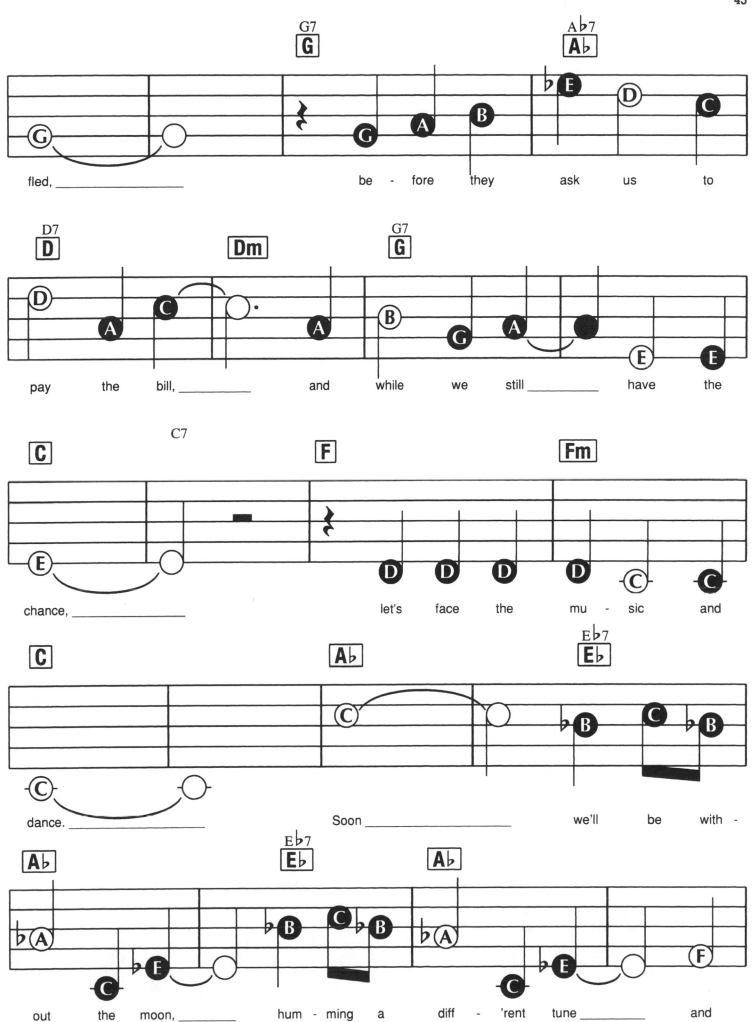

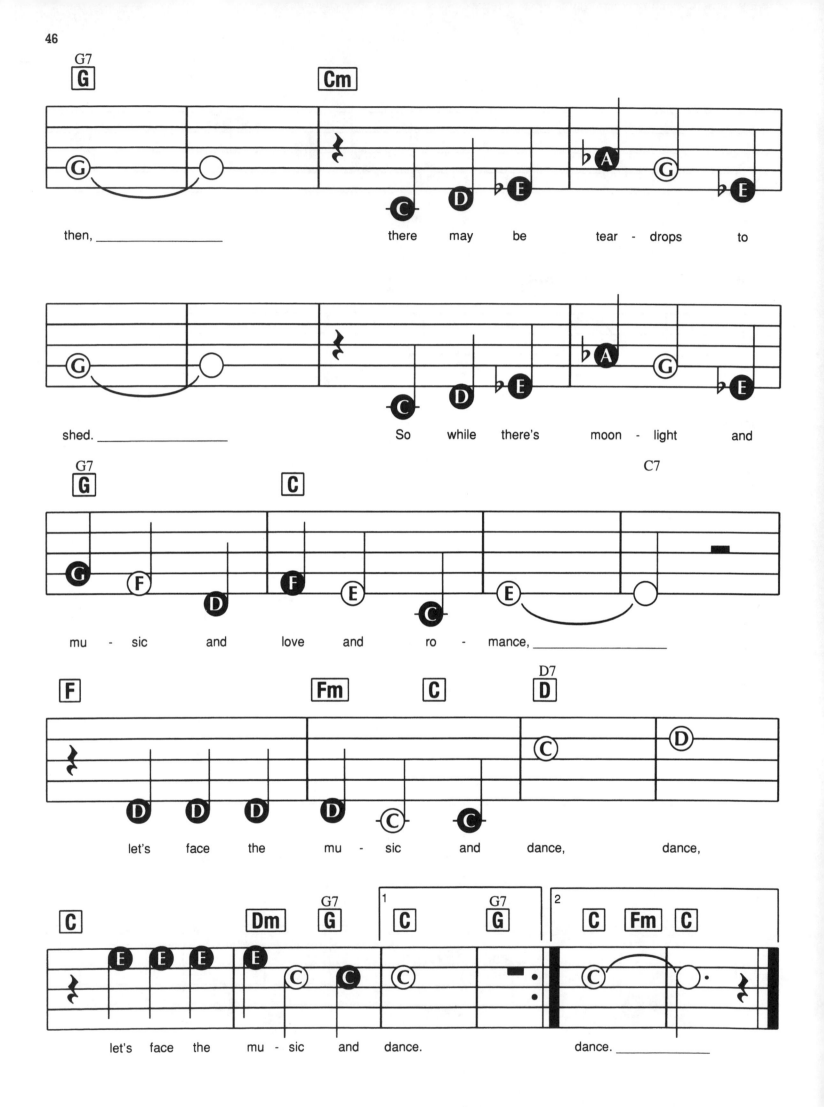

The Music of Goodbye
from OUT OF AFRICA

Registration 1
Rhythm: Ballad or Rock

Words and Music by John Barry,
Alan Bergman and Marilyn Bergman

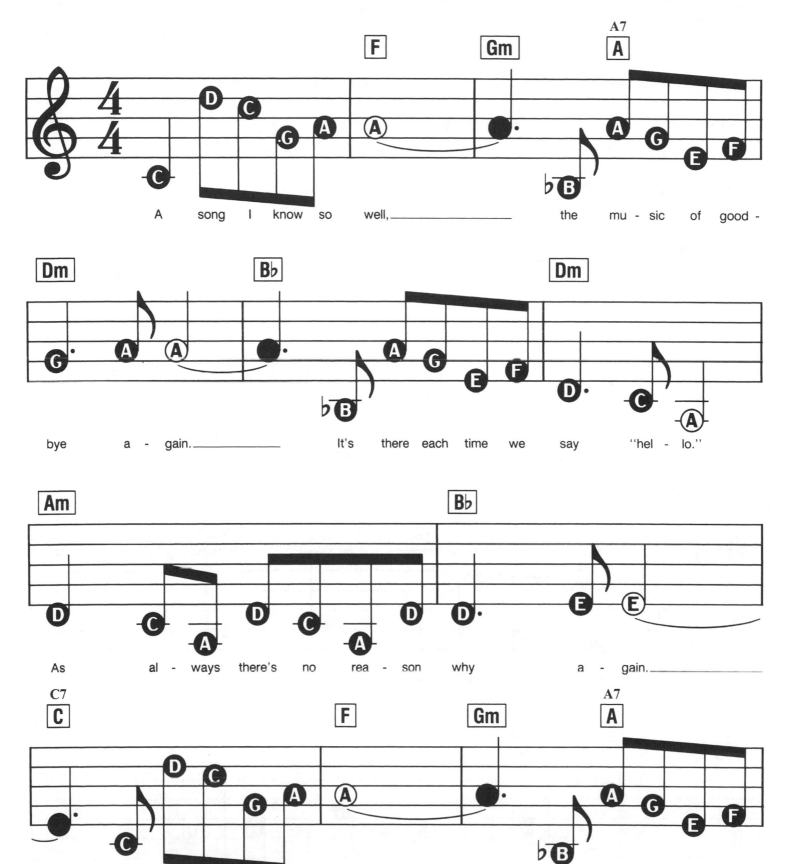

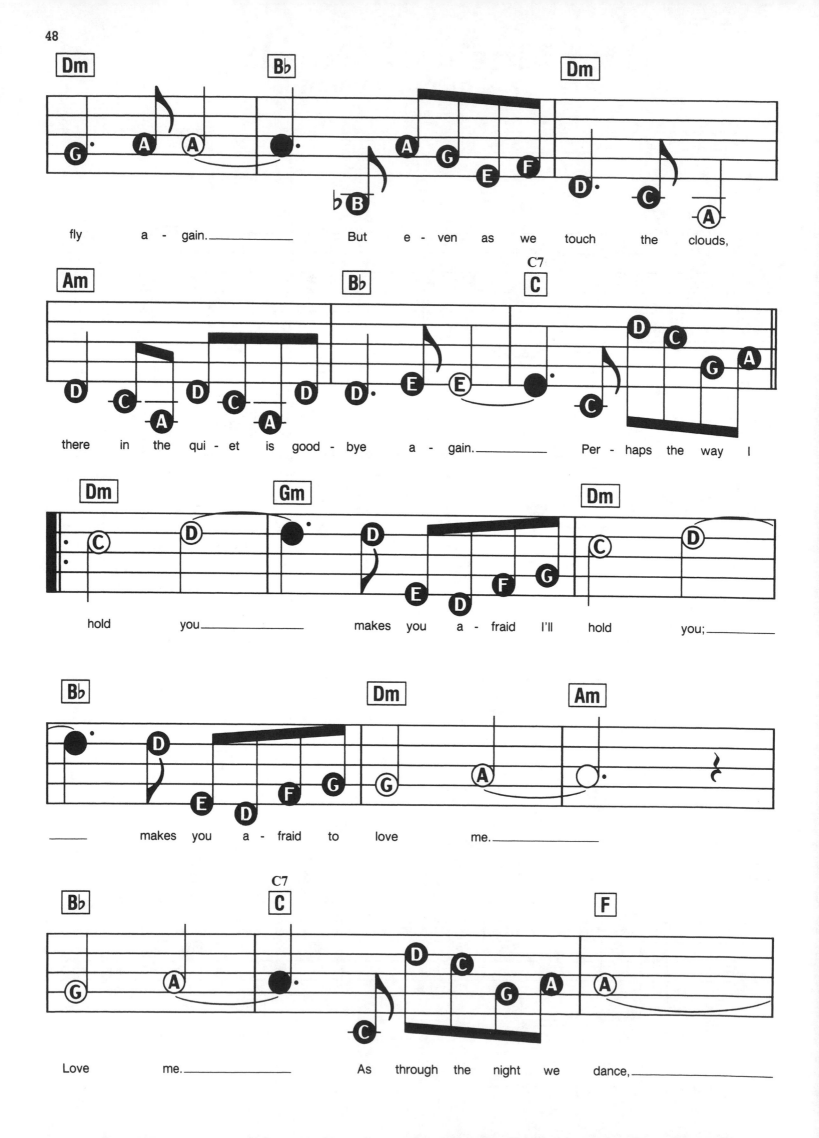

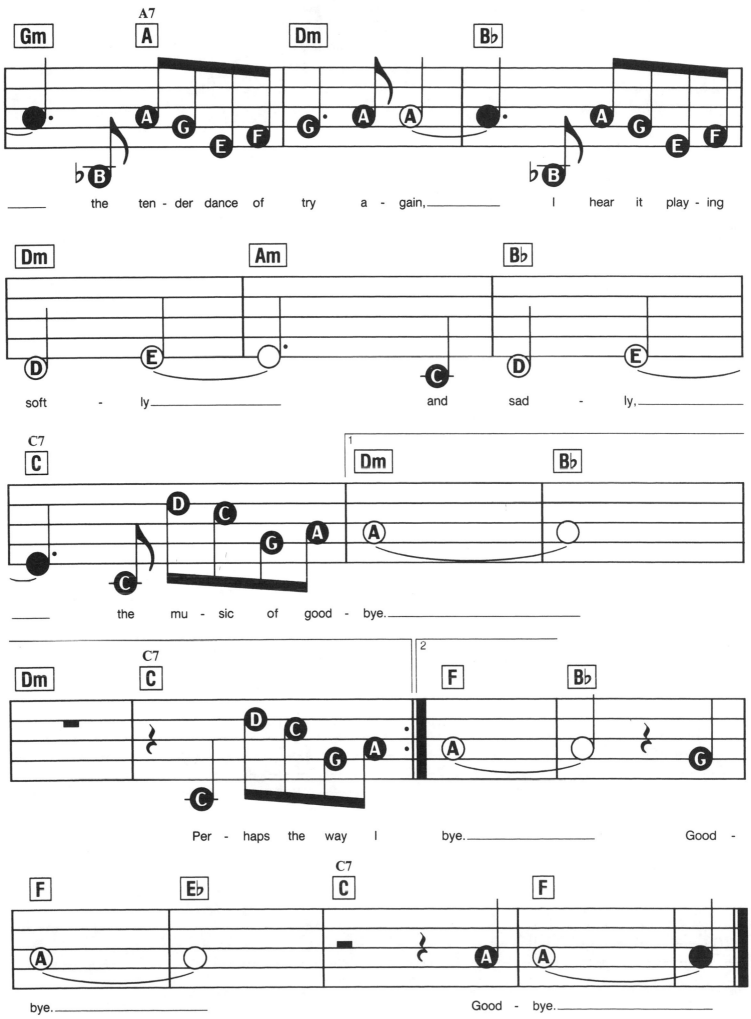

Long Ago
(And Far Away)
from COVER GIRL

Registration 3
Rhythm: Ballad or Swing

Words by Ira Gershwin
Music by Jerome Kern

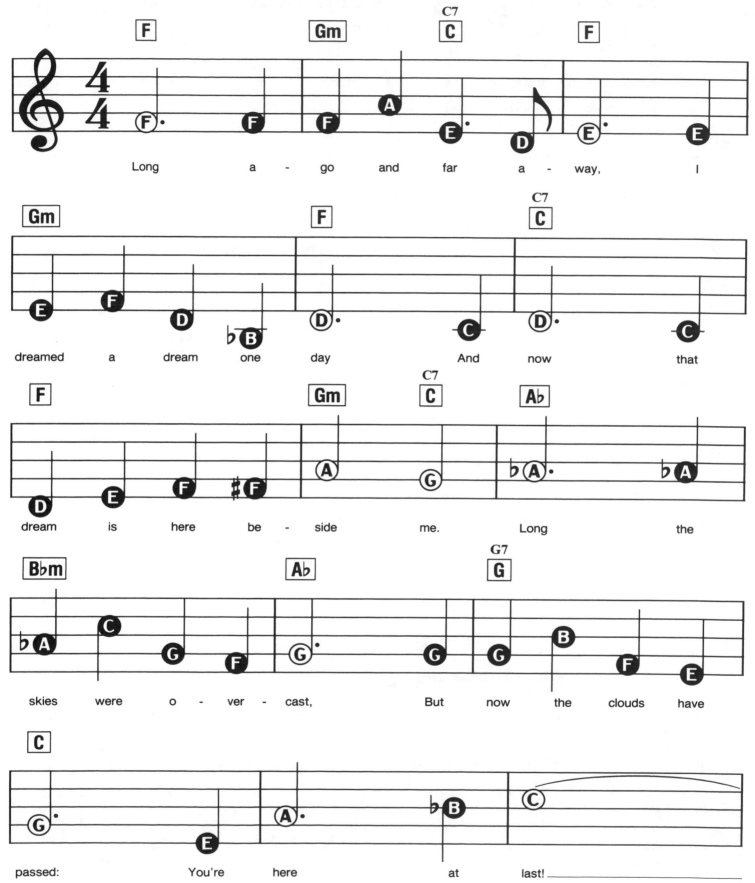

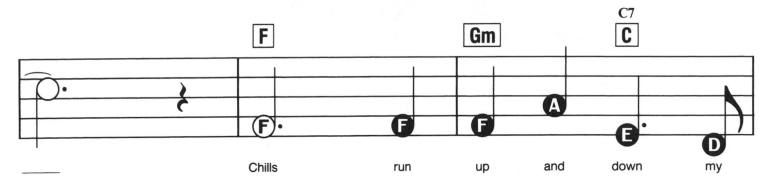

Chills run up and down my

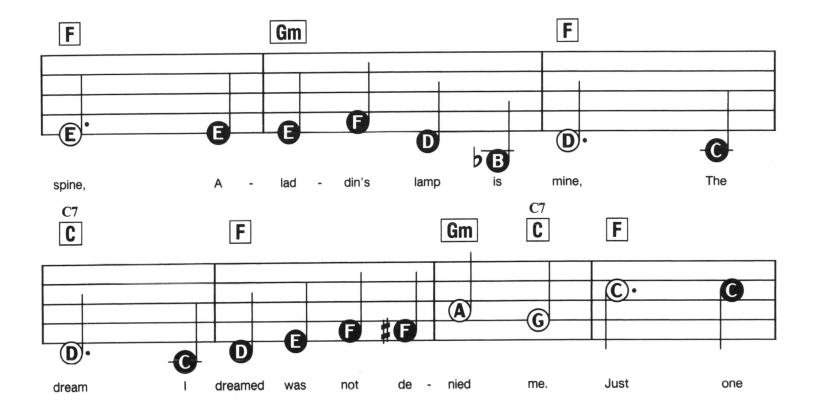

spine, A - lad - din's lamp is mine, The

dream I dreamed was not de - nied me. Just one

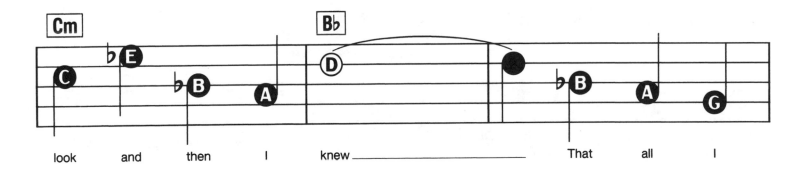

look and then I knew _____ That all I

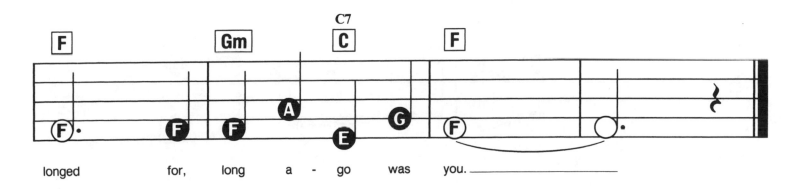

longed for, long a - go was you. _____

Mona Lisa
from the Paramount Picture CAPTAIN CAREY, U.S.A.

Registration 9
Rhythm: Swing or Ballad

Words and Music by Jay Livingston
and Ray Evans

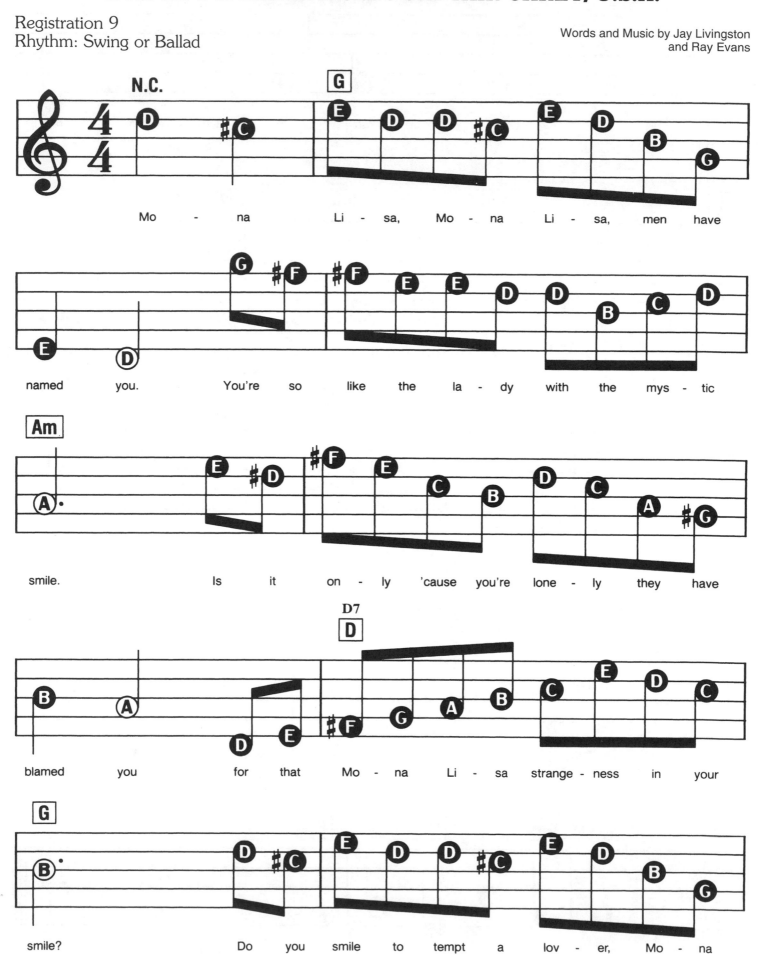

53

Moonlight Becomes You
from the Paramount Picture ROAD TO MOROCCO

Registration 1
Rhythm: Swing or Ballad

Words by Johnny Burke
Music by James Van Heusen

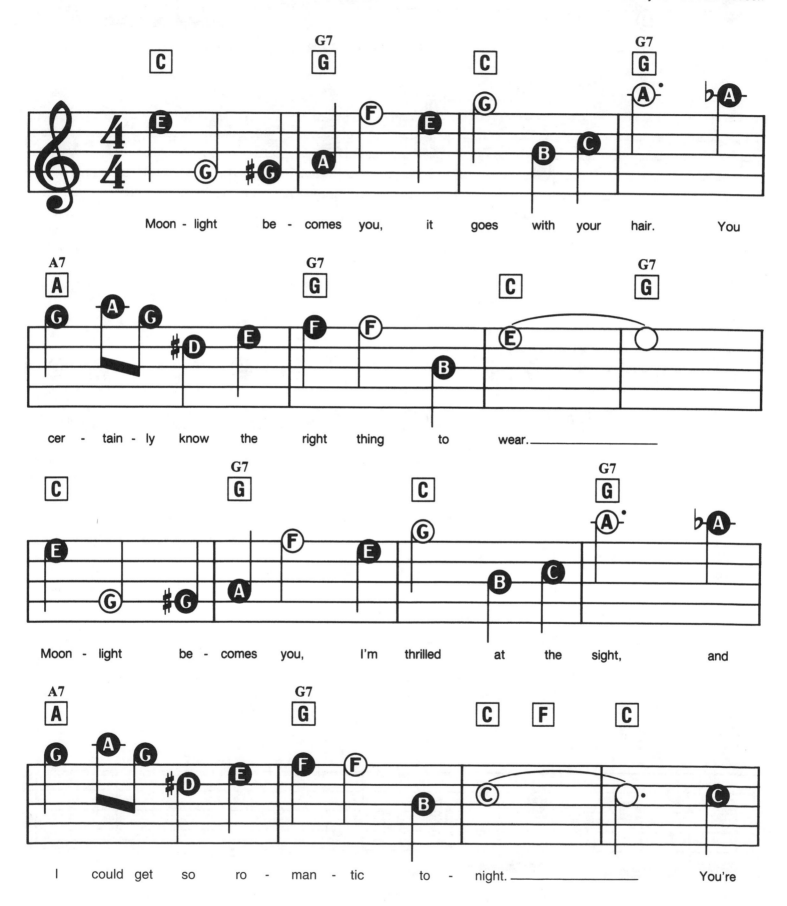

The Nearness of You
from the Paramount Picture ROMANCE IN THE DARK

Registration 9
Rhythm: Ballad or Fox Trot

Words by Ned Washington
Music by Hoagy Carmichael

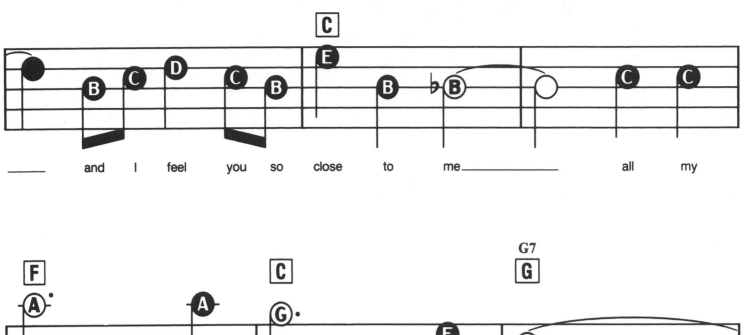

_____ and I feel you so close to me_____ all my

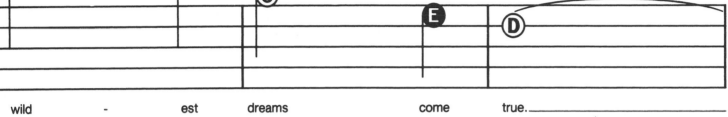

wild - est dreams come true._____

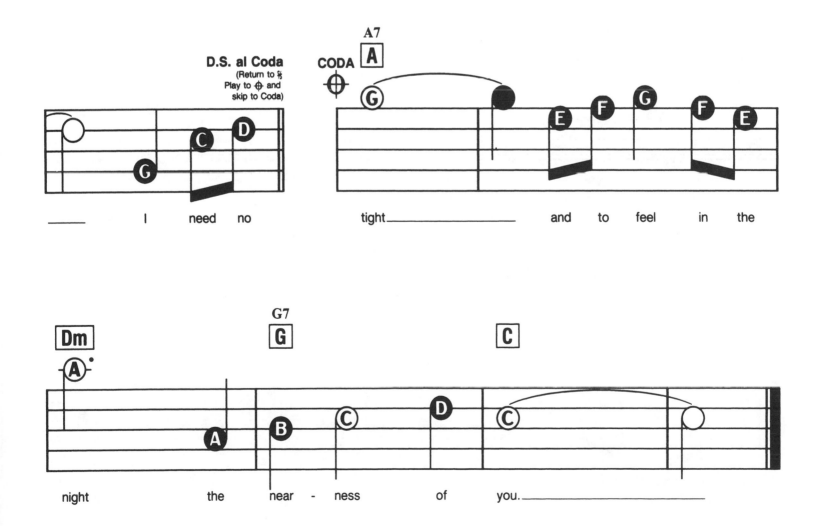

_____ I need no

tight_____ and to feel in the

night the near - ness of you._____

Raindrops Keep Fallin' on My Head

from BUTCH CASSIDY AND THE SUNDANCE KID

Registration 1
Rhythm: 8-Beat or Swing

Lyric by Hal David
Music by Burt Bacharach

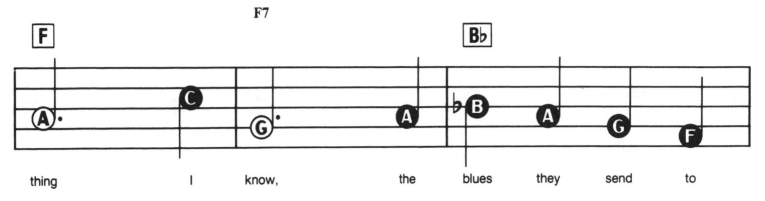

thing I know, the blues they send to

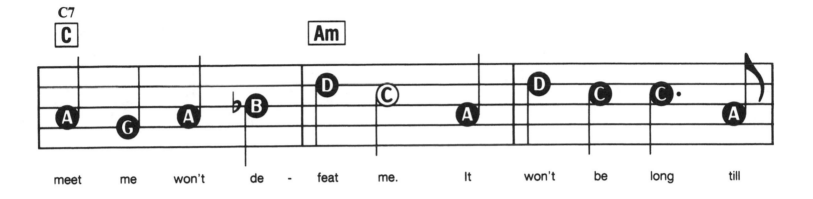

meet me won't de - feat me. It won't be long till

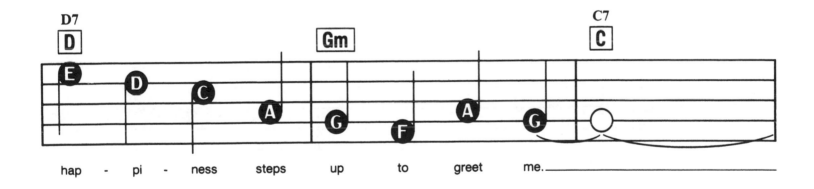

hap - pi - ness steps up to greet me._____

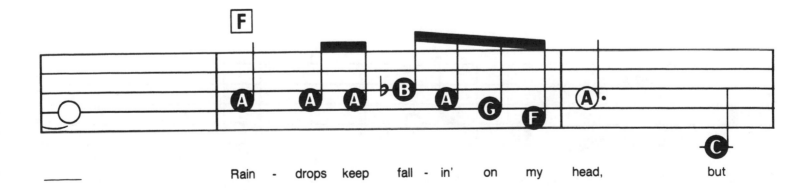

_____ Rain - drops keep fall - in' on my head, but

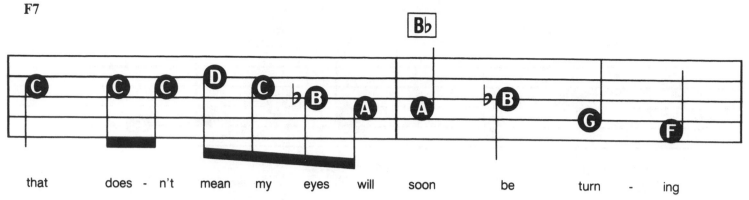

that does - n't mean my eyes will soon be turn - ing

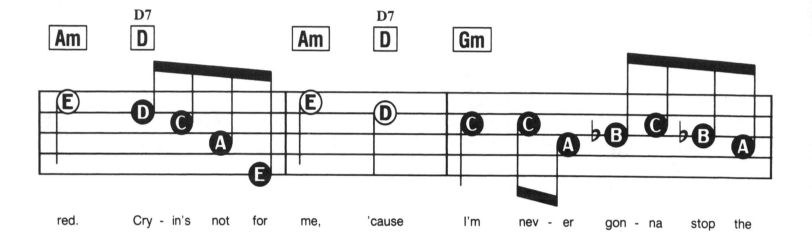

red. Cry - in's not for me, 'cause I'm nev - er gon - na stop the

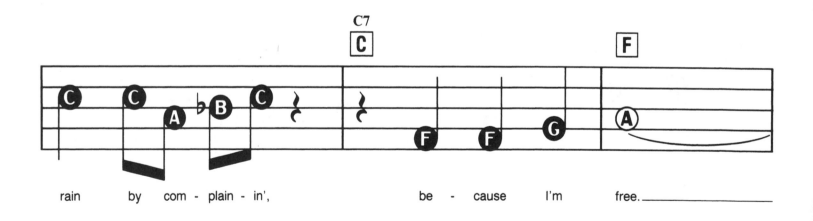

rain by com - plain - in', be - cause I'm free. _____

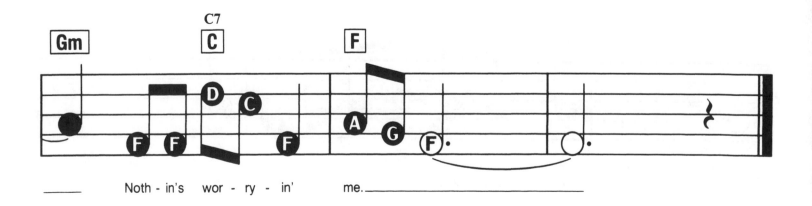

_____ Noth - in's wor - ry - in' me. _____

Somewhere Out There
from AN AMERICAN TAIL

Registration 3
Rhythm: Ballad or 8-Beat

Music by Barry Mann and James Horner
Lyric by Cynthia Weil

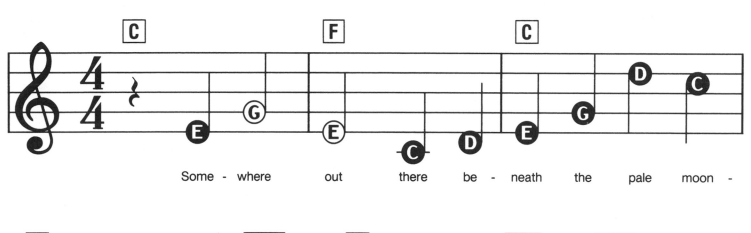

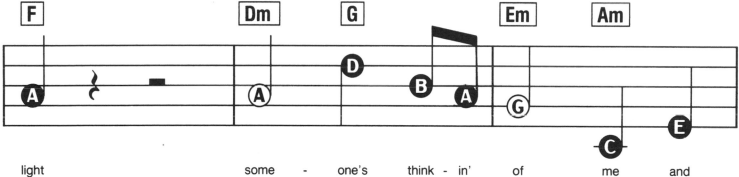

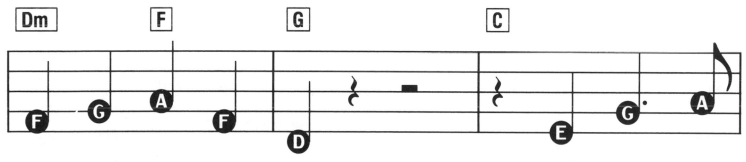

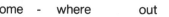

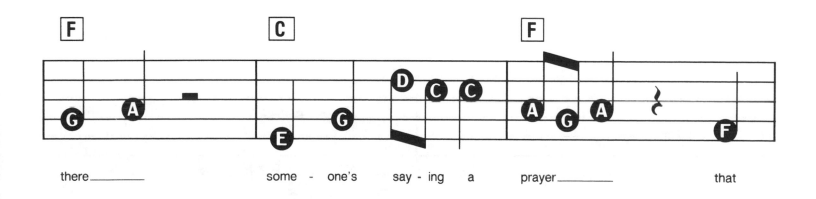

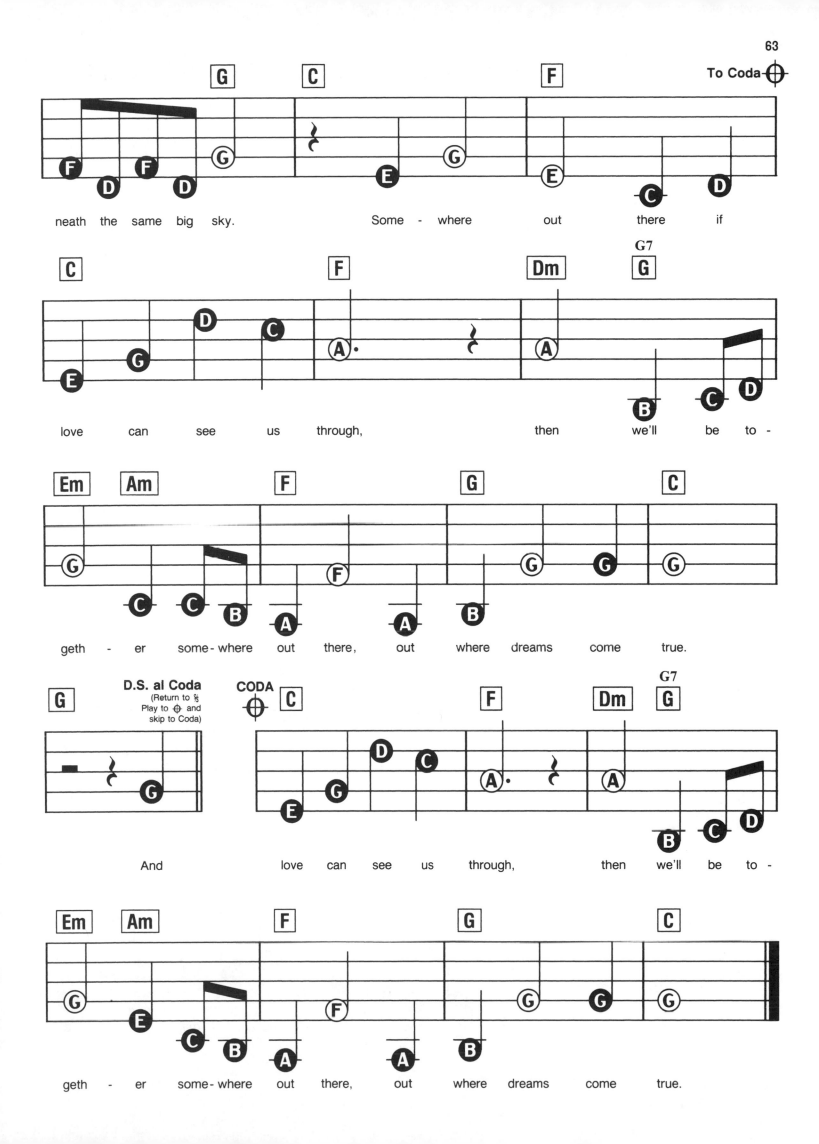

Ready to Take a Chance Again

from the Paramount Picture FOUL PLAY

Registration 1
Rhythm: Pop/Rock or 8-Beat

Words by Norman Gimbel
Music by Charles Fox

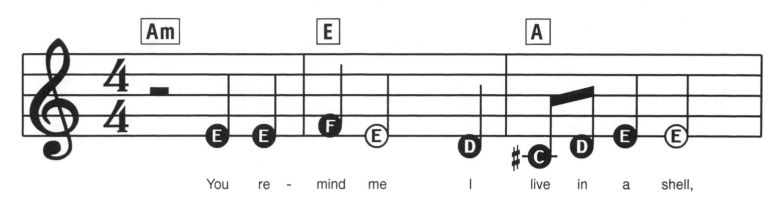

You re - mind me I live in a shell,

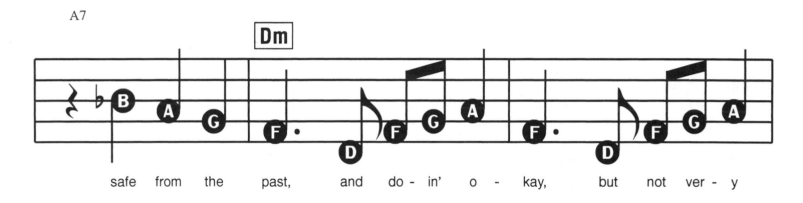

safe from the past, and do - in' o - kay, but not ver - y

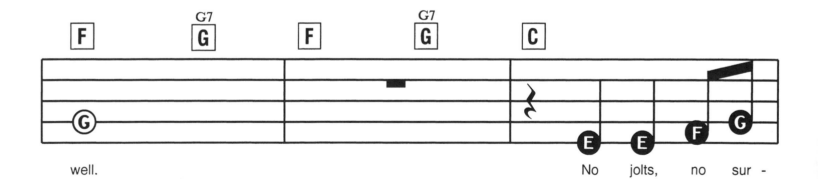

well. No jolts, no sur -

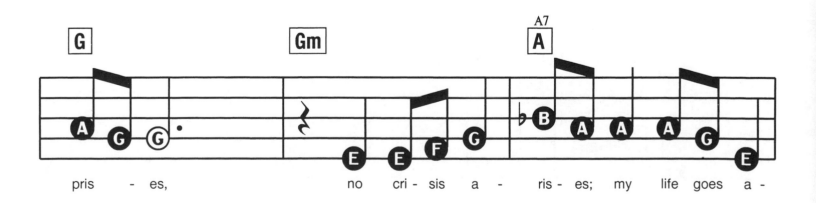

pris - es, no cri - sis a - ris - es; my life goes a -

long as it should, it's all ver-y nice, but not ver-y good._____

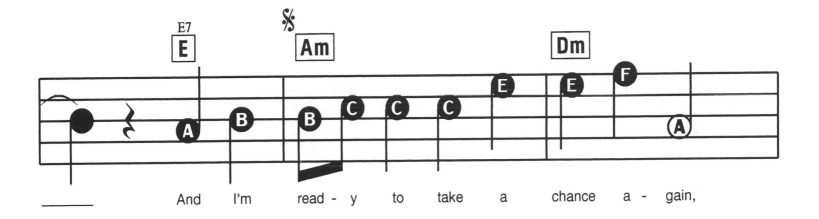

_____ And I'm read-y to take a chance a-gain,

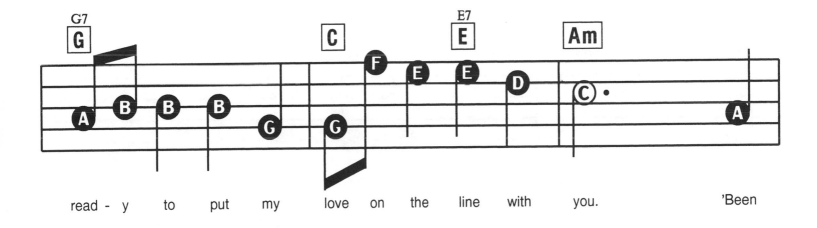

read-y to put my love on the line with you. 'Been

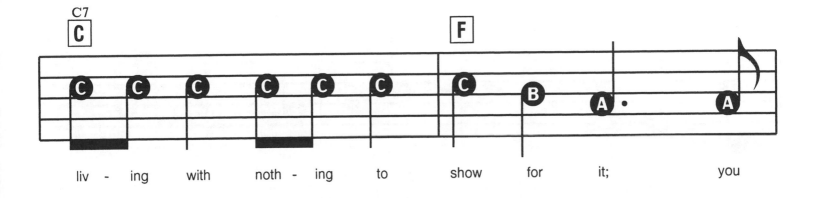

liv-ing with noth-ing to show for it; you

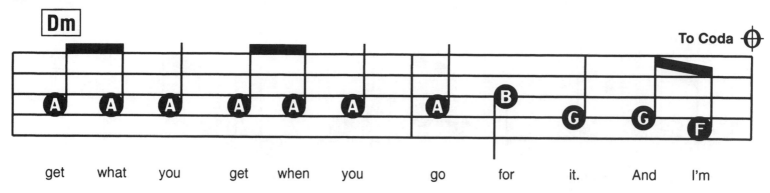

To Coda ⊕

get   what   you   get   when   you   go   for   it.   And   I'm

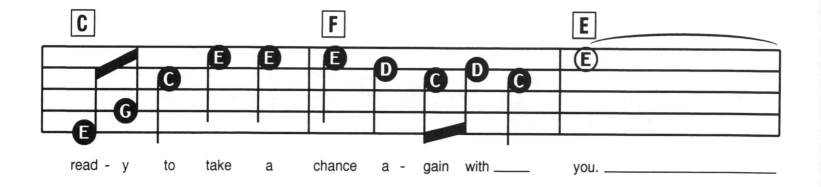

read - y   to   take   a   chance   a - gain   with _____   you. _____

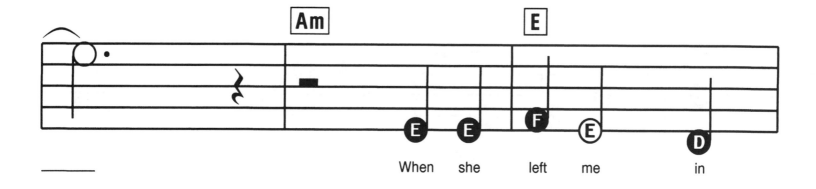

_____   When   she   left   me   in

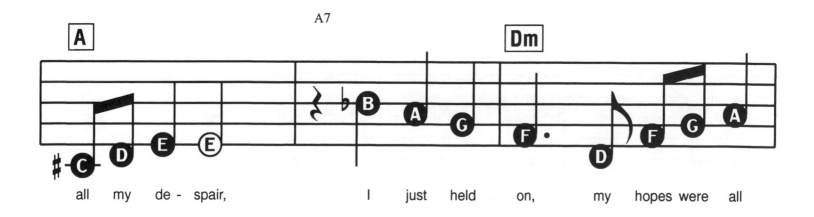

all   my   de - spair,   I   just   held   on,   my   hopes   were   all

D.S. al Coda
(Return to %
Play to ⊕ and
Skip to Coda)

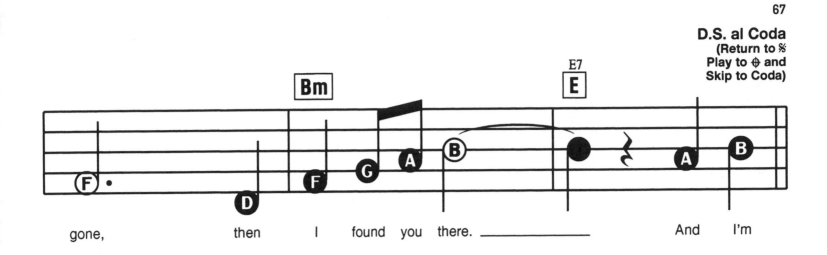

gone,   then   I   found you   there. _____   And   I'm

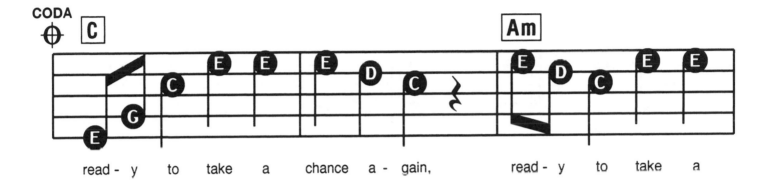

read - y to take   a   chance a - gain,   read - y   to   take   a

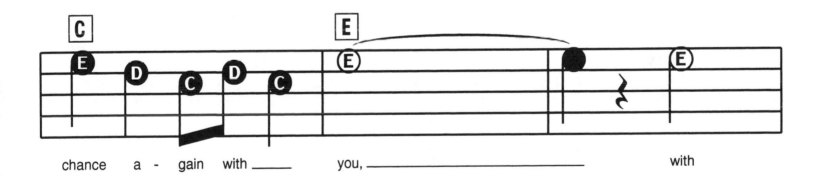

chance   a - gain with ____   you, _____   with

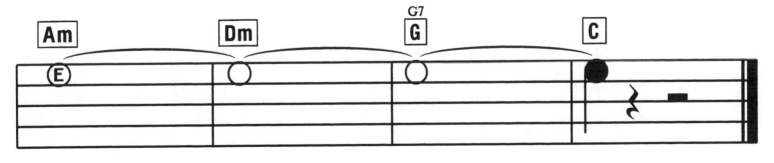

you. _____

Sea of Love
featured in the Motion Picture SEA OF LOVE

Registration 7
Rhythm: Slow Rock

Words and Music by George Khoury
and Philip Baptiste

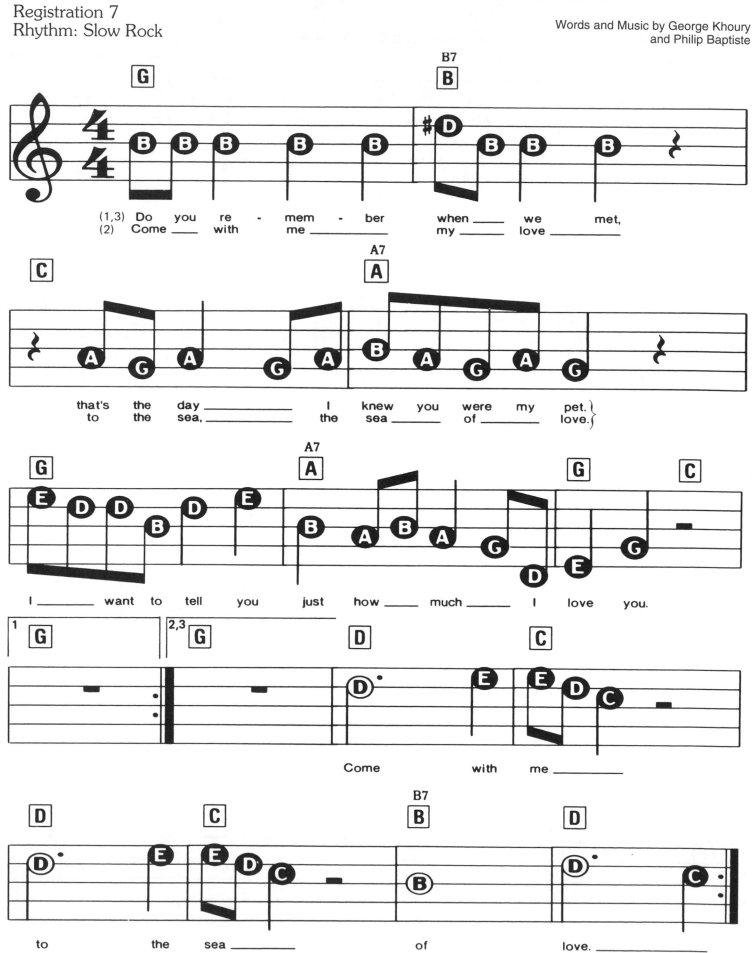

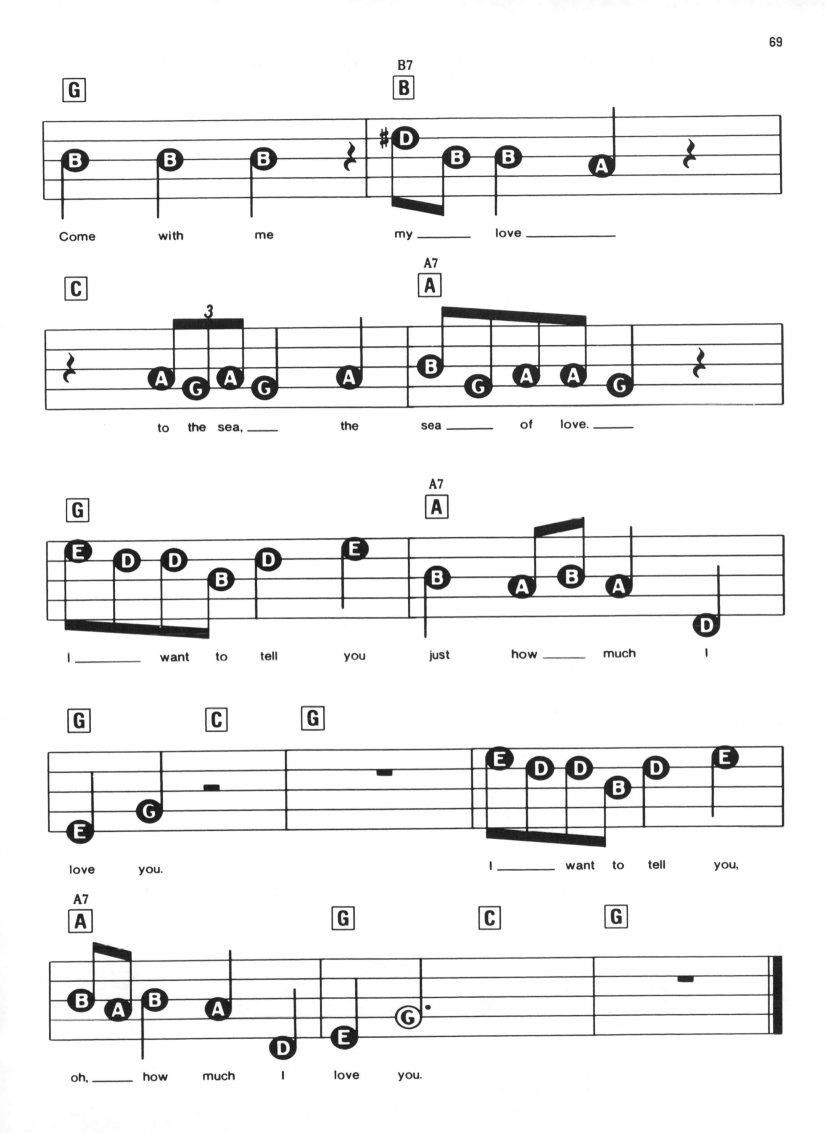

Somewhere in My Memory

from the Twentieth Century Fox Motion Picture HOME ALONE

Registration 3
Rhythm: Ballad

Words by Leslie Bricusse
Music by John Williams

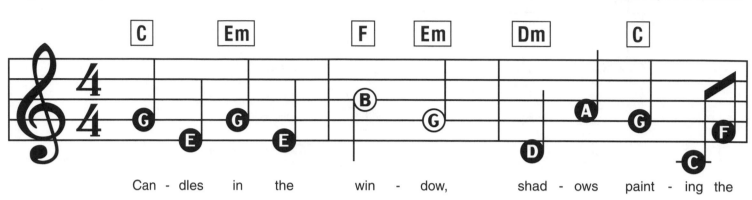

Can - dles in the win - dow, shad - ows paint - ing the

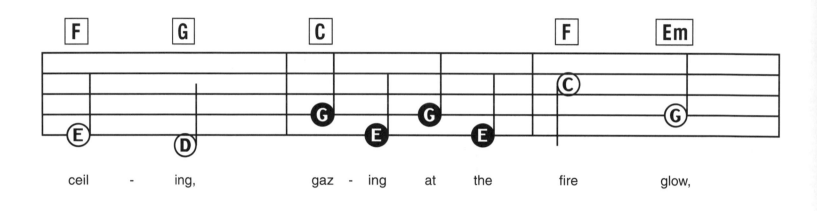

ceil - ing, gaz - ing at the fire glow,

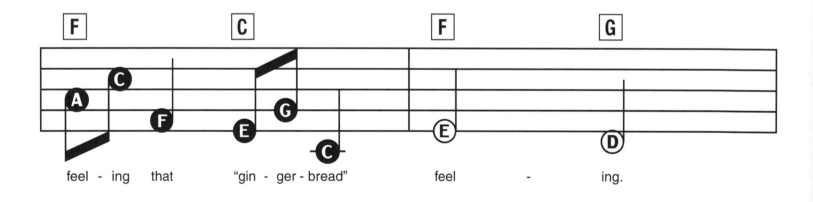

feel - ing that "gin - ger - bread" feel - ing.

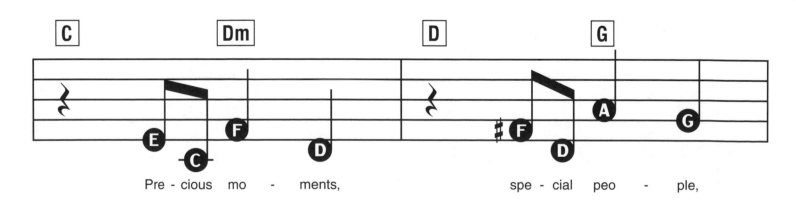

Pre - cious mo - ments, spe - cial peo - ple,

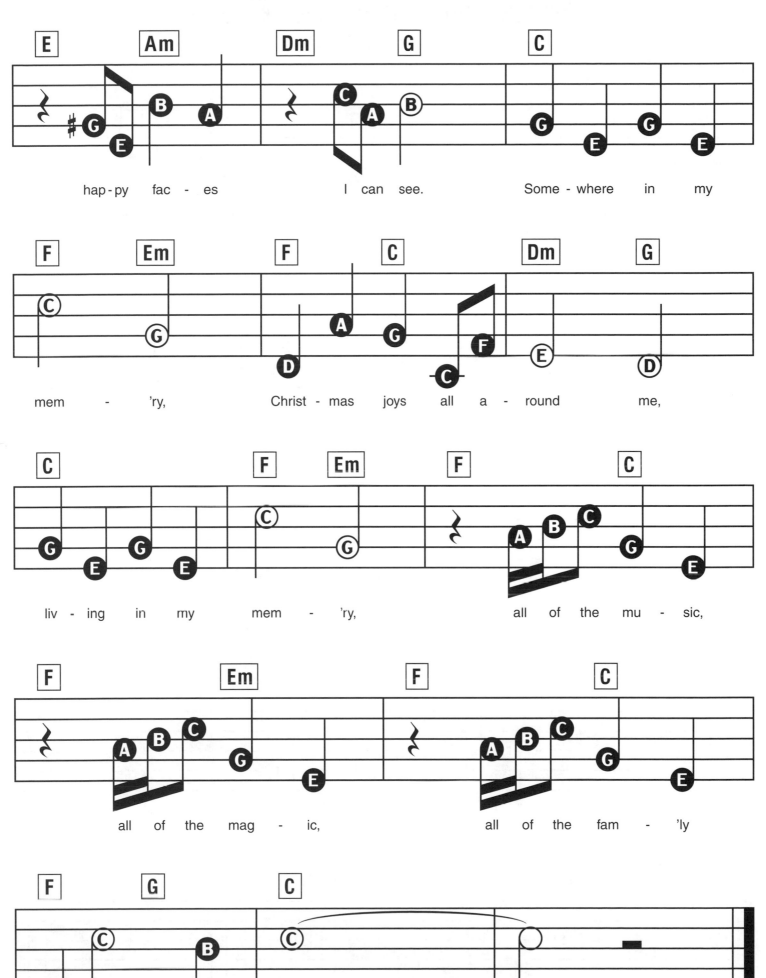

Somewhere in Time
from SOMEWHERE IN TIME

Registration 3
Rhythm: Ballad

By John Barry

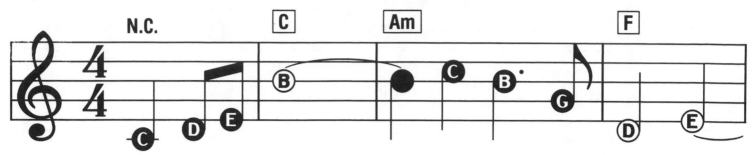

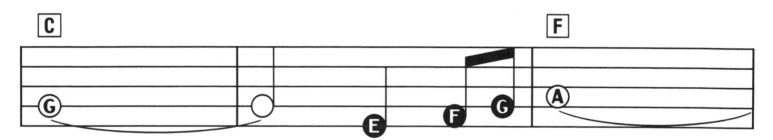

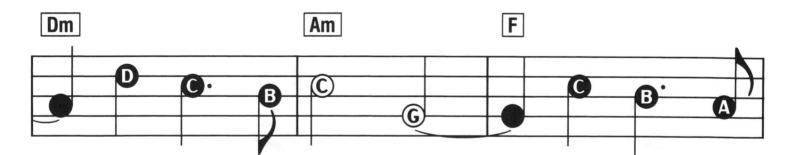

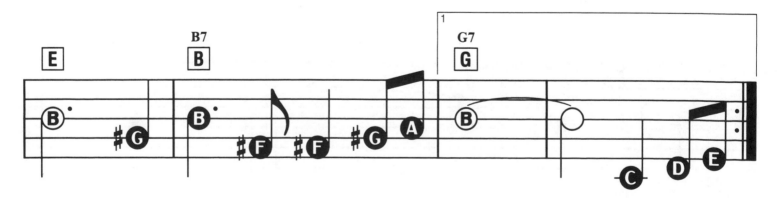

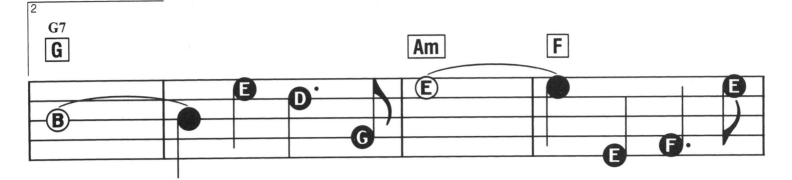

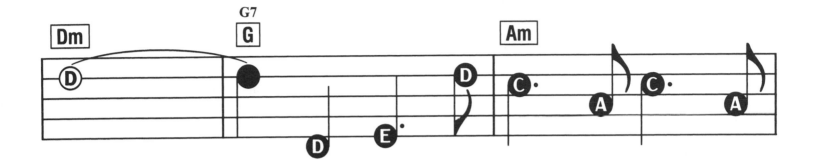

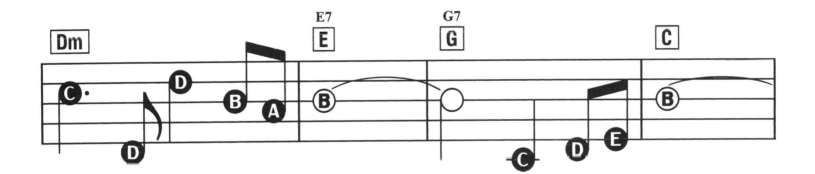

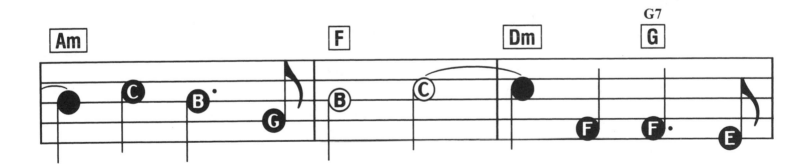

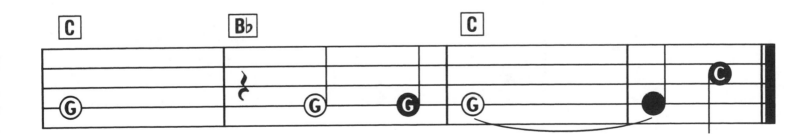

Thanks for the Memory
from the Paramount Picture THE BIG BROADCAST OF 1938

Registration 3
Rhythm: Swing or Ballad

Words and Music by Leo Robin
and Ralph Rainger

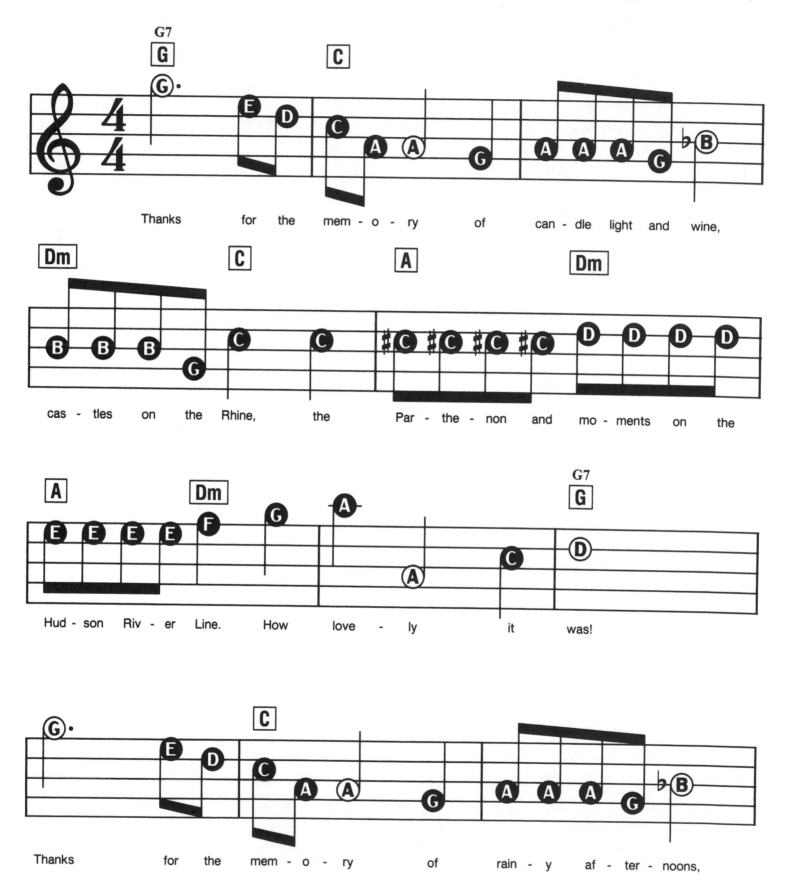

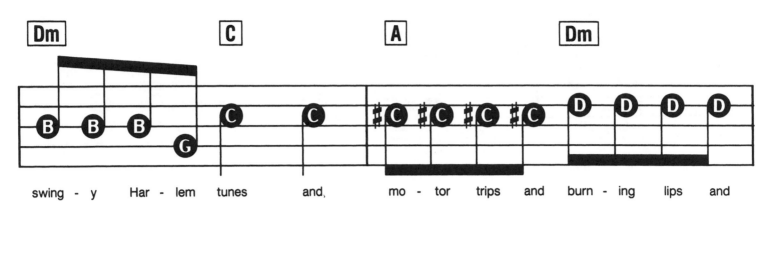

swing - y   Har - lem   tunes   and,   mo - tor   trips   and   burn - ing   lips   and

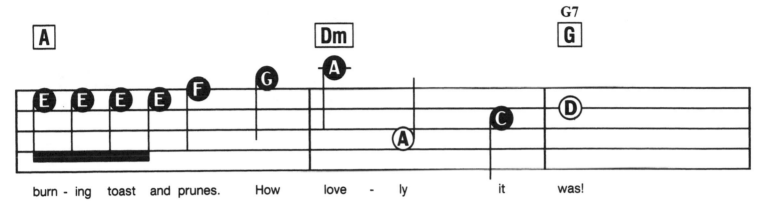

burn - ing   toast   and   prunes.   How   love - ly   it   was!

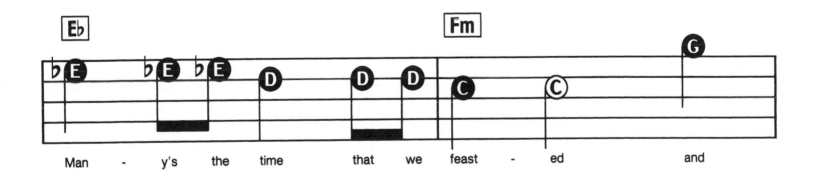

Man - y's   the   time   that   we   feast - ed   and

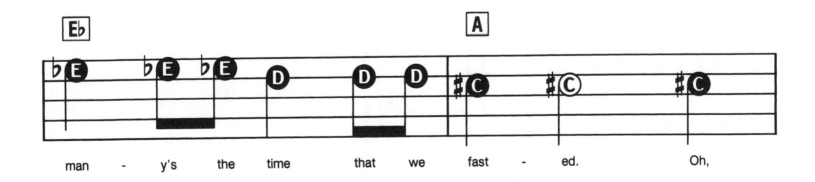

man - y's   the   time   that   we   fast - ed.   Oh,

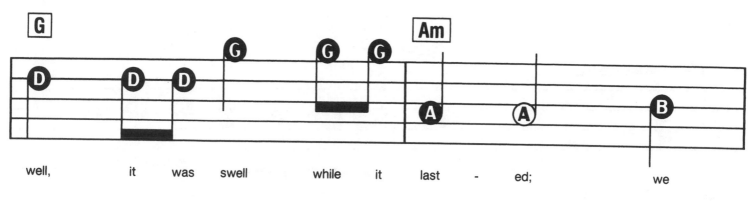

well, it was swell while it last - ed; we

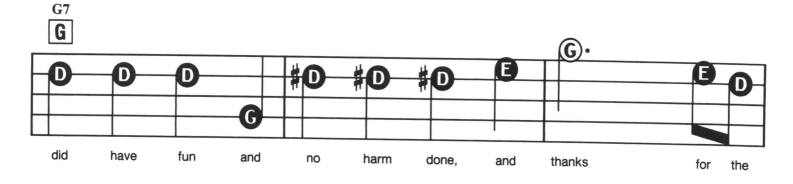

did have fun and no harm done, and thanks for the

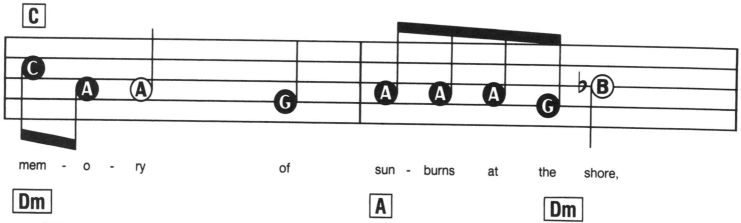

mem - o - ry of sun - burns at the shore,

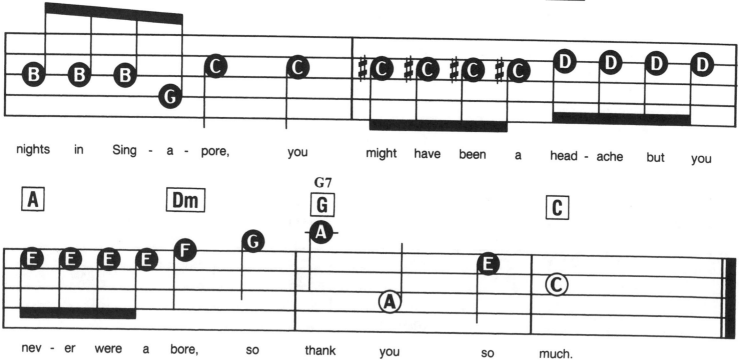

nights in Sing - a - pore, you might have been a head - ache but you

nev - er were a bore, so thank you so much.

Three Coins in the Fountain
from THREE COINS IN THE FOUNTAIN

Registration 2
Rhythm: Swing or Ballad

Words by Sammy Cahn
Music by Jule Styne

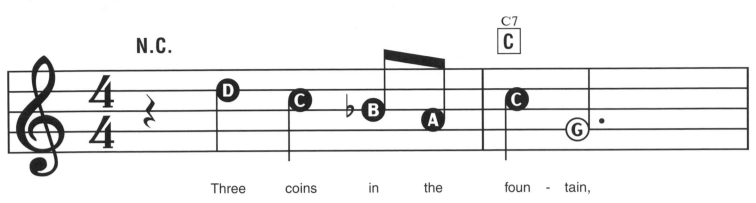

Three coins in the foun - tain,

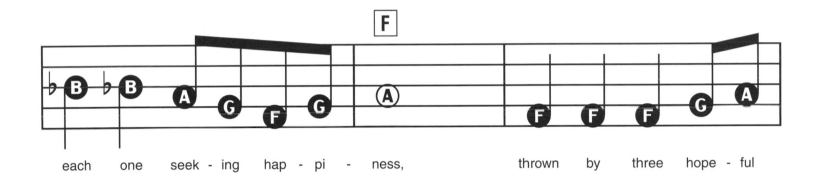

each one seek - ing hap - pi - ness, thrown by three hope - ful

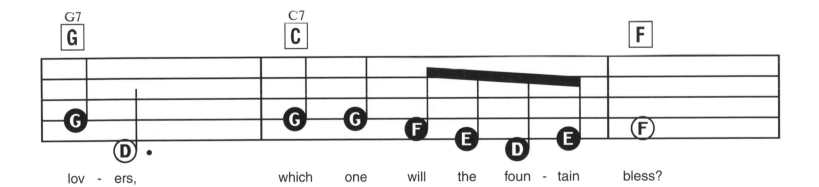

lov - ers, which one will the foun - tain bless?

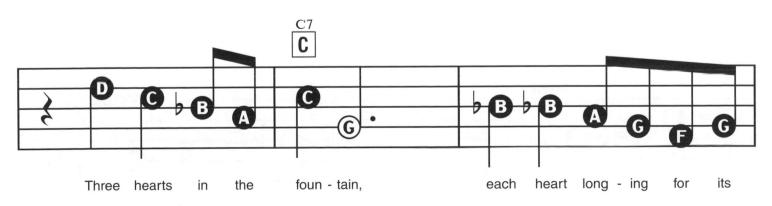

Three hearts in the foun - tain, each heart long - ing for its

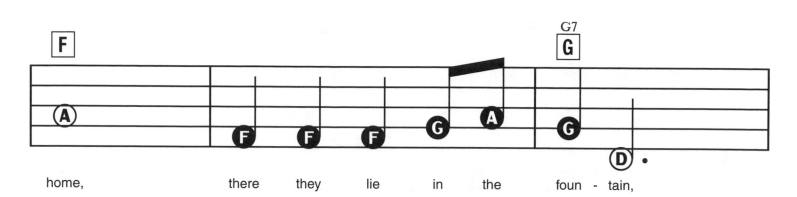

home, there they lie in the foun - tain,

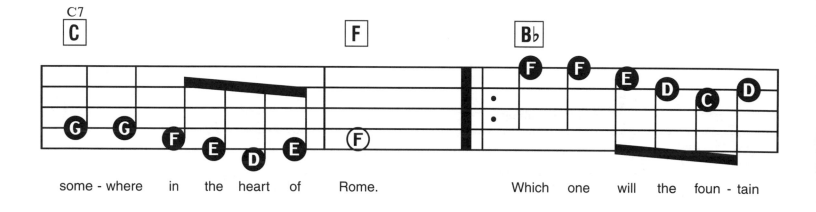

some - where in the heart of Rome. Which one will the foun - tain

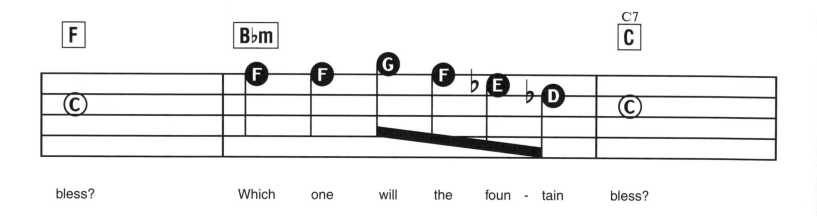

bless? Which one will the foun - tain bless?

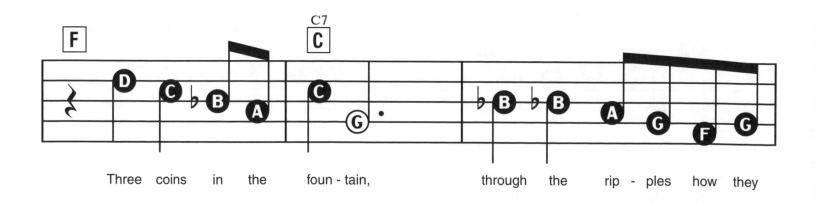

Three coins in the foun - tain, through the rip - ples how they

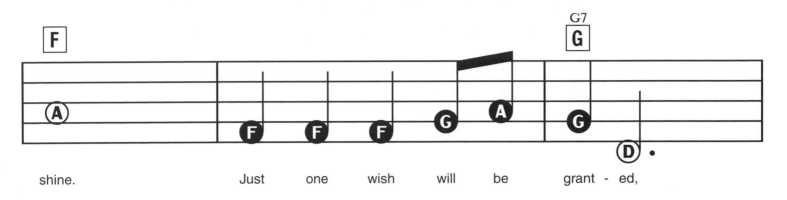

shine.　　Just　one　wish　will　be　grant - ed,

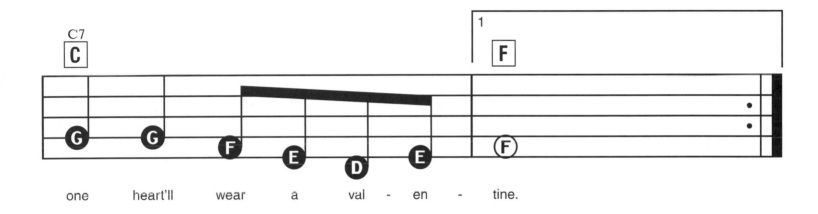

one　heart'll　wear　a　val - en - tine.

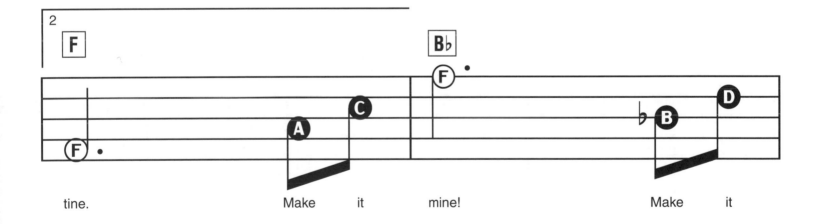

tine.　　Make　it　mine!　　Make　it

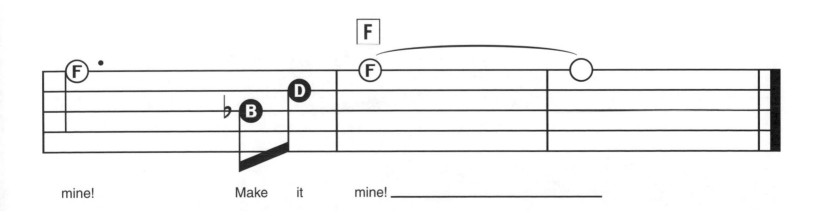

mine!　　Make　it　mine! _____

Watch What Happens
from THE UMBRELLAS OF CHERBOURG

Registration 2
Rhythm: Bossa Nova or Latin

Music by Michel Legrand
Original French Text by Jacques Demy
English Lyrics by Norman Gimbel

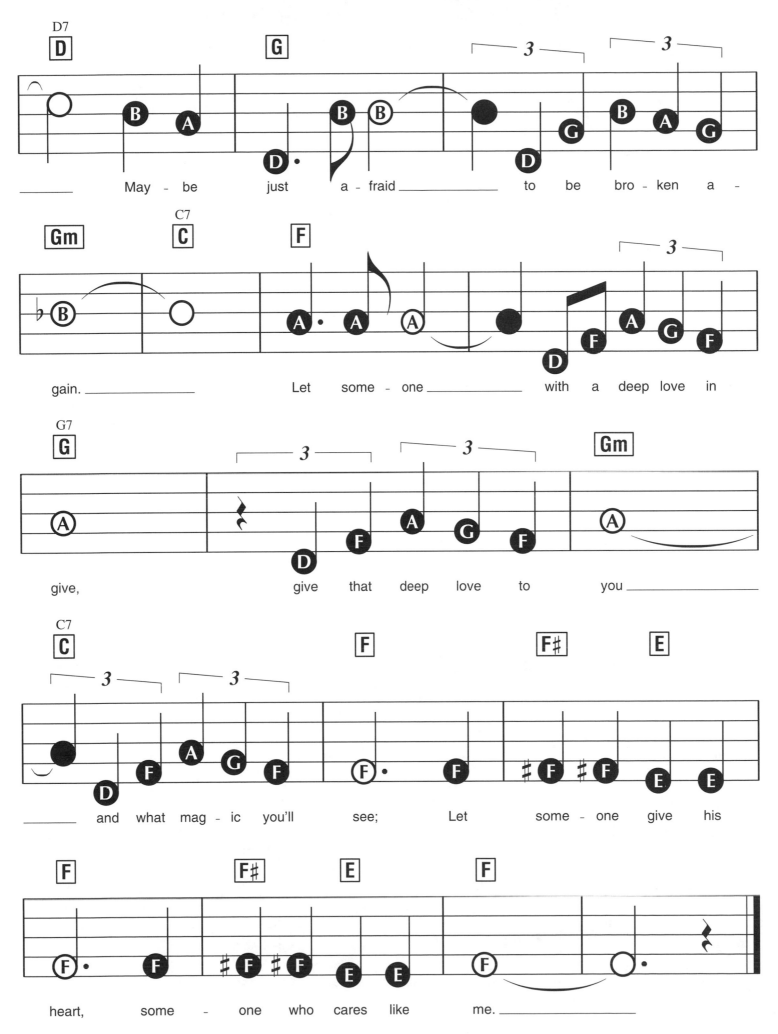

The Way We Were
from the Motion Picture THE WAY WE WERE

Registration 8
Rhythm: Slow Rock or Ballad

Words by Alan and Marilyn Bergman
Music by Marvin Hamlisch

Mem - 'ries, _____ light the cor - ners of my mind,
pic - tures, _____ of the smiles we left be - hind
Mem - 'ries, _____ may be beau - ti - ful and yet;

Mist - y wa - ter - co - lor mem - 'ries   of the way   we
Smiles we gave to one an - oth - er,   for the way   we
what's too pain - ful to re - mem - ber

were.   Scat - tered   were. _____

Can it be that it was all so sim - ple then,   or has time re - writ - ten ev - 'ry

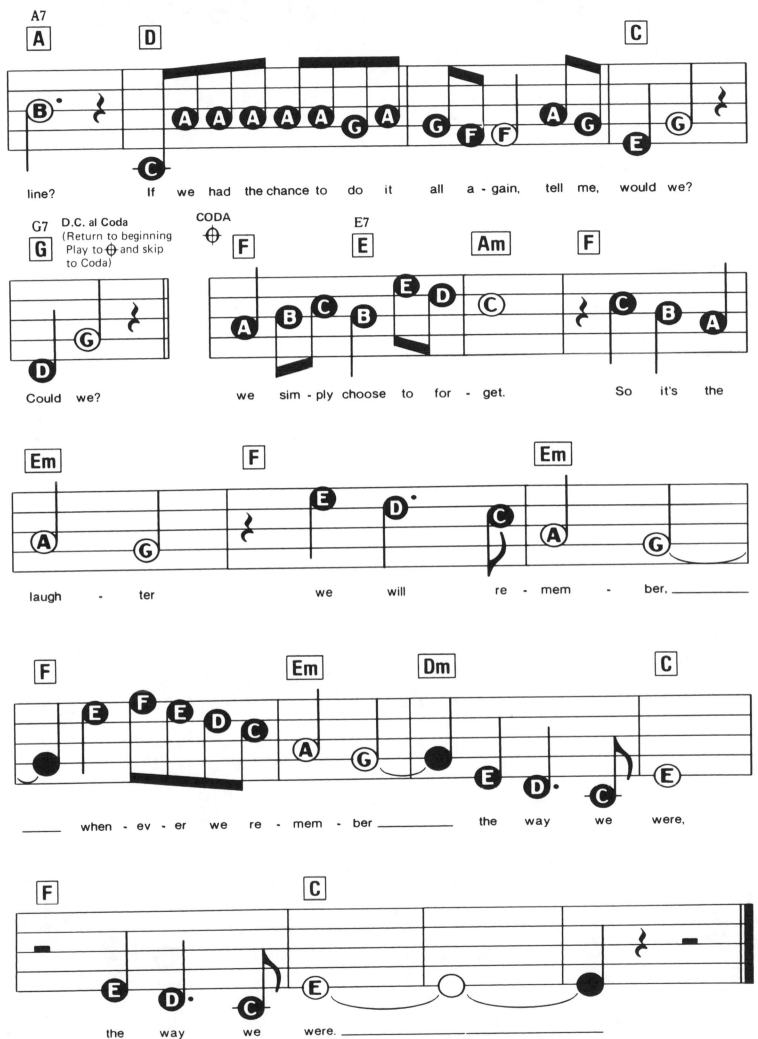

The Way You Look Tonight
from SWING TIME

Registration 1
Rhythm: Fox Trot or Ballad

Words by Dorothy Fields
Music by Jerome Kern

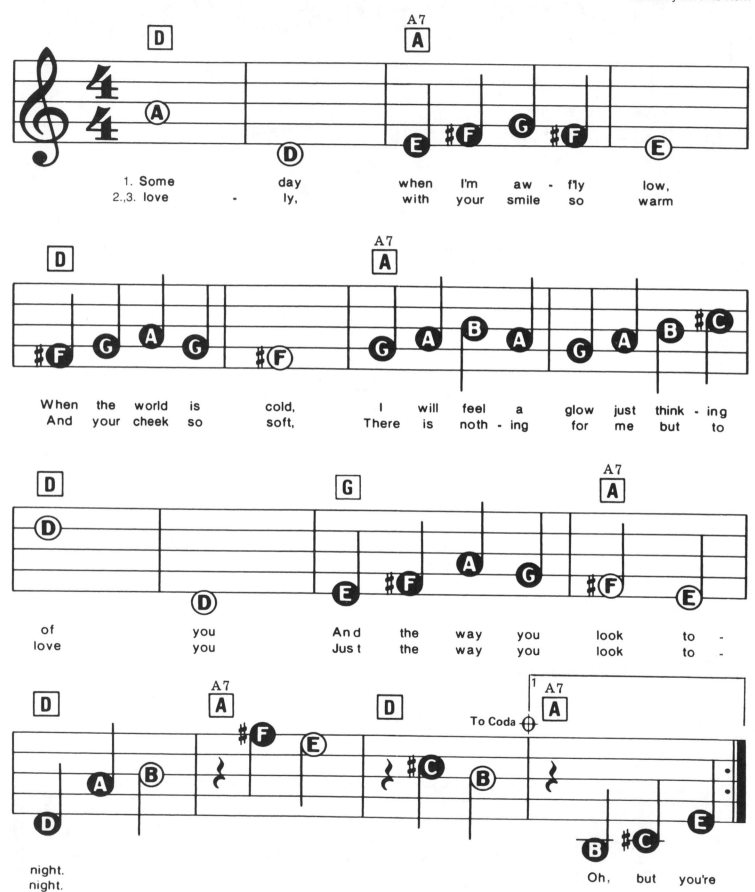

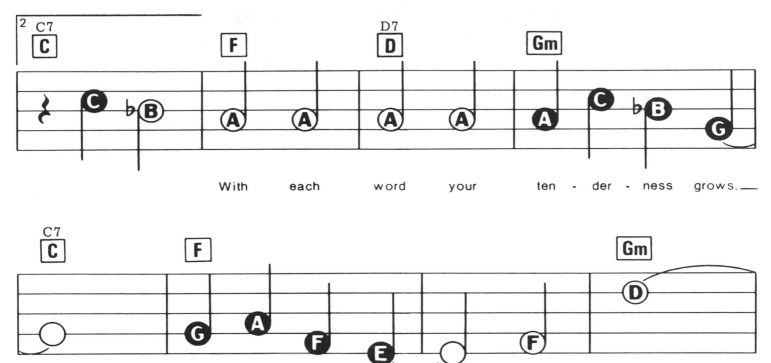

With each word your ten - der - ness grows.

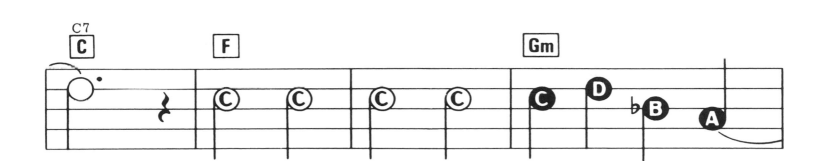

tear - ing my fear a - part,

And that laugh that wrin - kles your nose

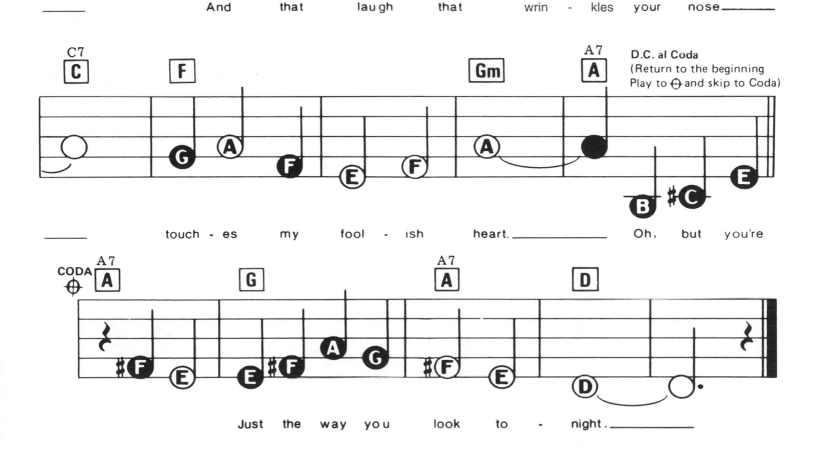

touch - es my fool - ish heart. Oh, but you're

D.C. al Coda
(Return to the beginning
Play to ⊕ and skip to Coda)

CODA

Just the way you look to - night.

When I Fall in Love

featured in the TriStar Motion Picture SLEEPLESS IN SEATTLE

Registration 3
Rhythm: Ballad or Fox Trot

Words by Edward Heyman
Music by Victor Young

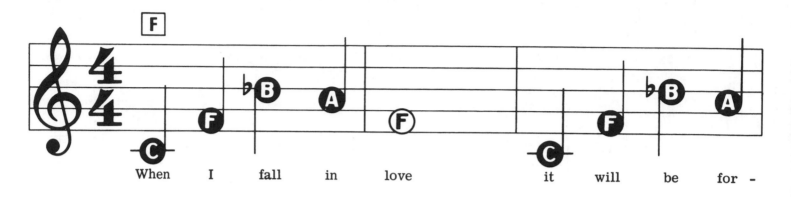

When I fall in love it will be for -

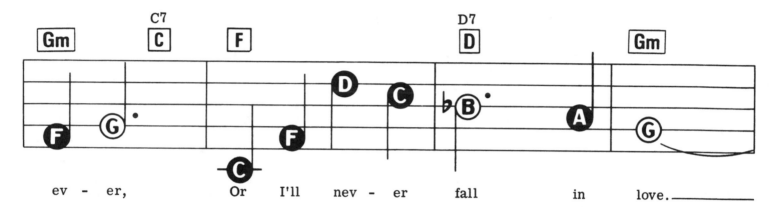

ev - er, Or I'll nev - er fall in love.

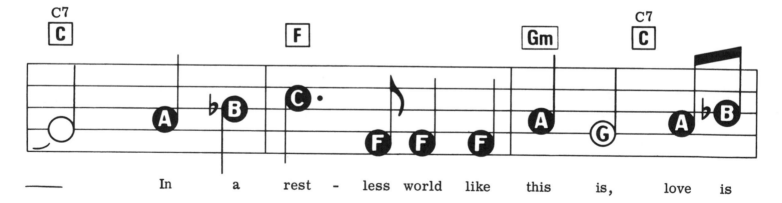

In a rest - less world like this is, love is

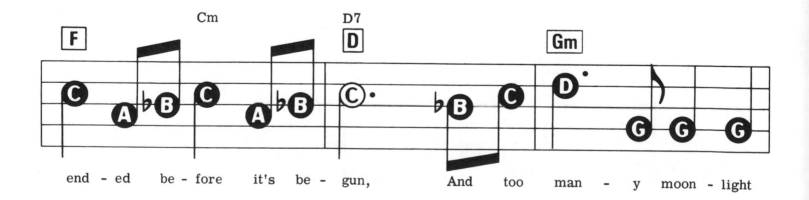

end - ed be - fore it's be - gun, And too man - y moon - light

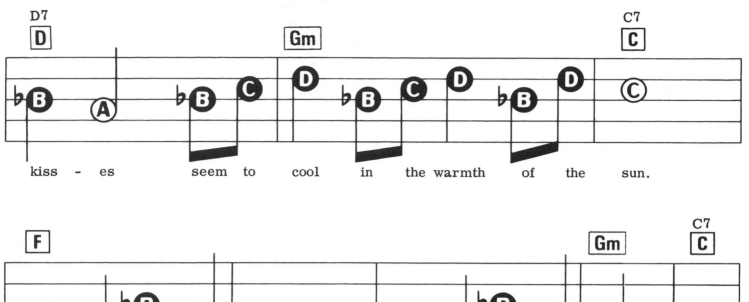

kiss - es seem to cool in the warmth of the sun.

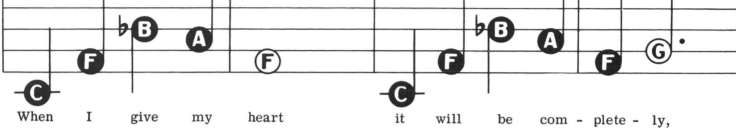

When I give my heart it will be com - plete - ly,

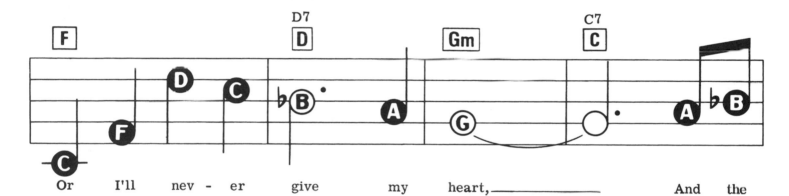

Or I'll nev - er give my heart,_____ And the

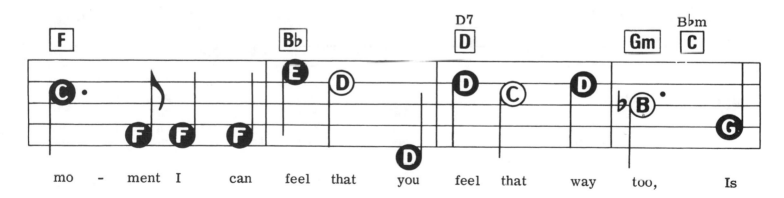

mo - ment I can feel that you feel that way too, Is

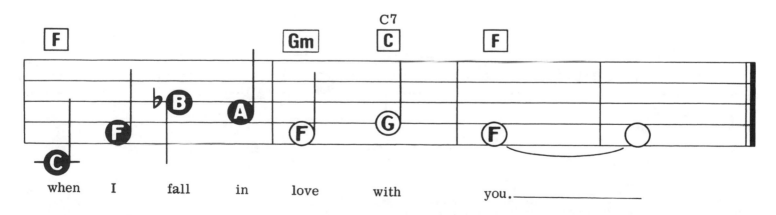

when I fall in love with you._____

Where Do I Begin

(Love Theme)
from the Paramount Picture LOVE STORY

Registration 8
Rhythm: Ballad

Words by Carl Sigman
Music by Francis Lai

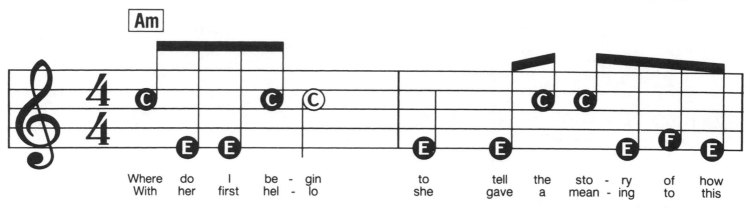

Where do I be - gin to tell the sto - ry of how
With her first hel - lo she gave a mean - ing to how this

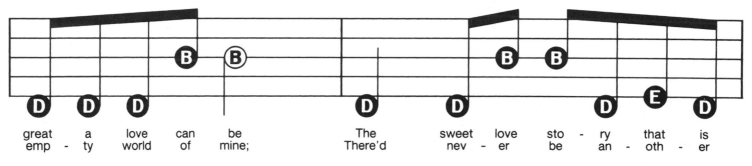

great a love can be mine; The sweet love sto - ry that is
emp - ty world of me; There'd nev - er be an - oth - er

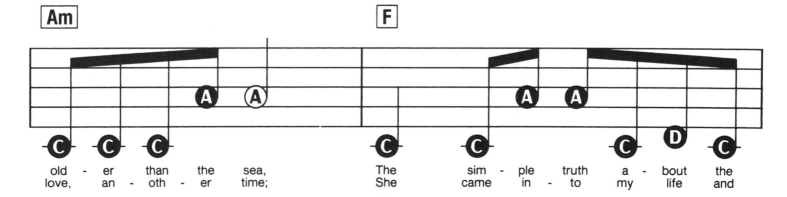

old - er than the sea, The sim - ple truth a - bout the
love, an - oth - er time; She came in - to my life and

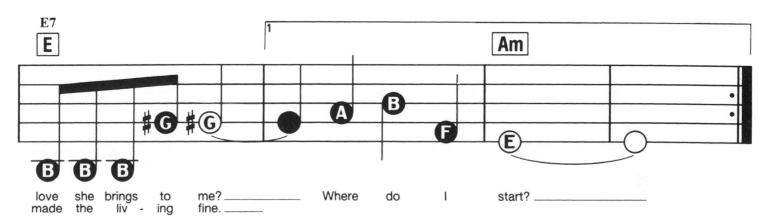

love she brings to me? Where do I start?
made the liv - ing fine.

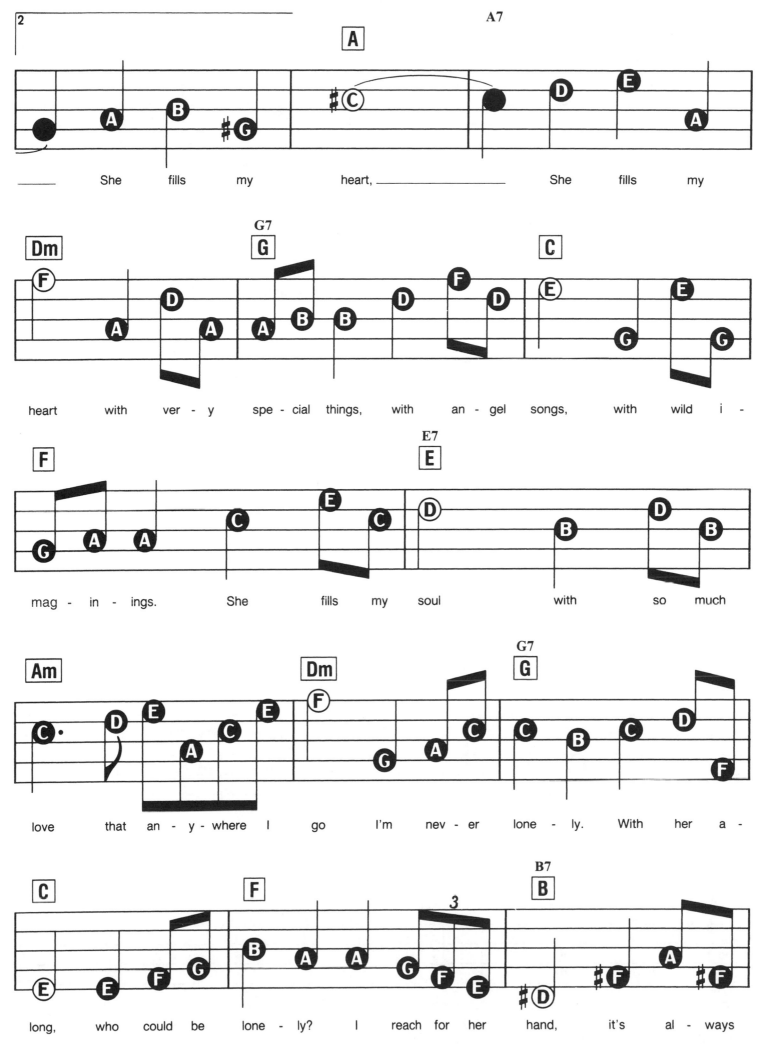

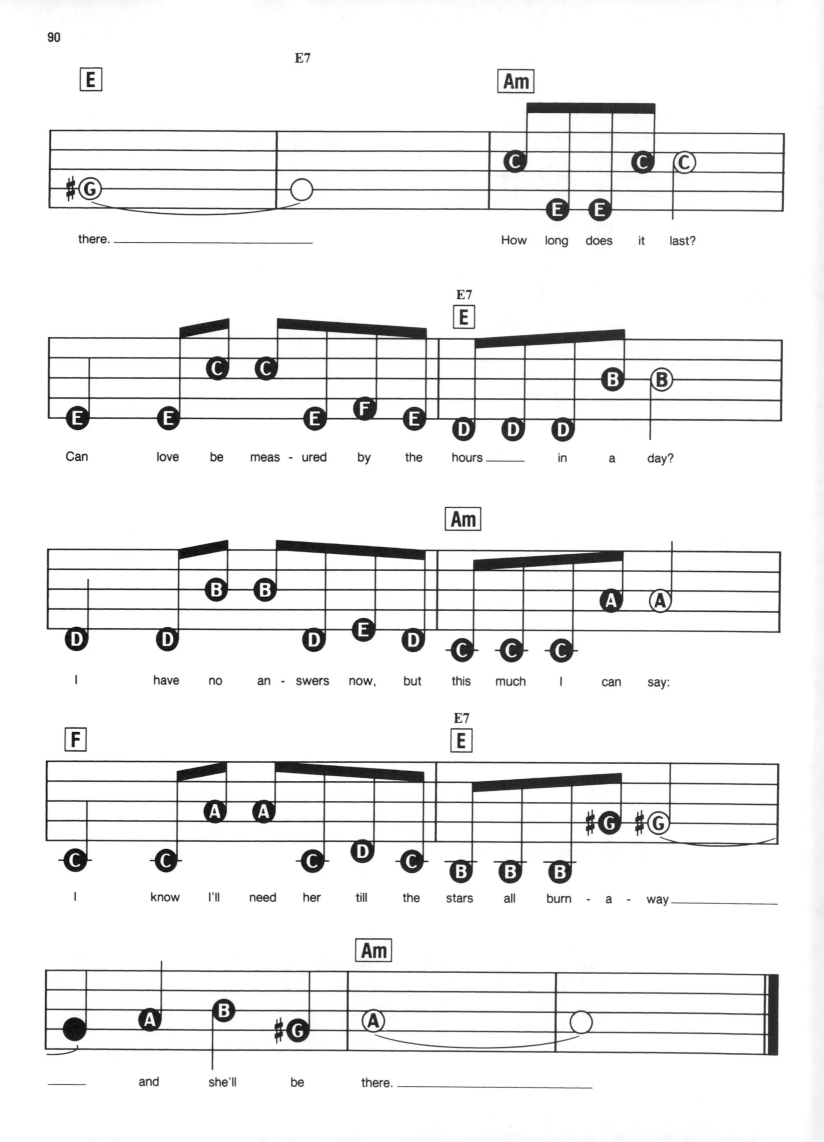

You Must Love Me
from the Cinergi Motion Picture EVITA

Registration 1
Rhythm: Pops

Words by Tim Rice
Music by Andrew Lloyd Webber

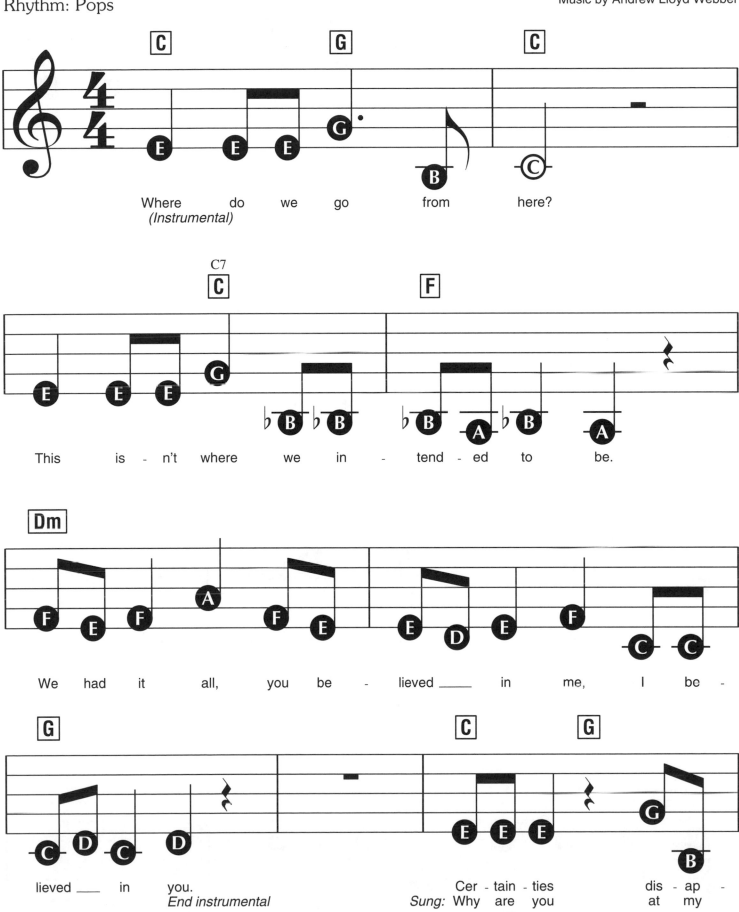

Where do we go from here?
(Instrumental)

This is - n't where we in - tend - ed to be.

We had it all, you be - lieved ____ in me, I be -

lieved ____ in you.
End instrumental

Cer - tain - ties dis - ap -
Sung: Why are you at my

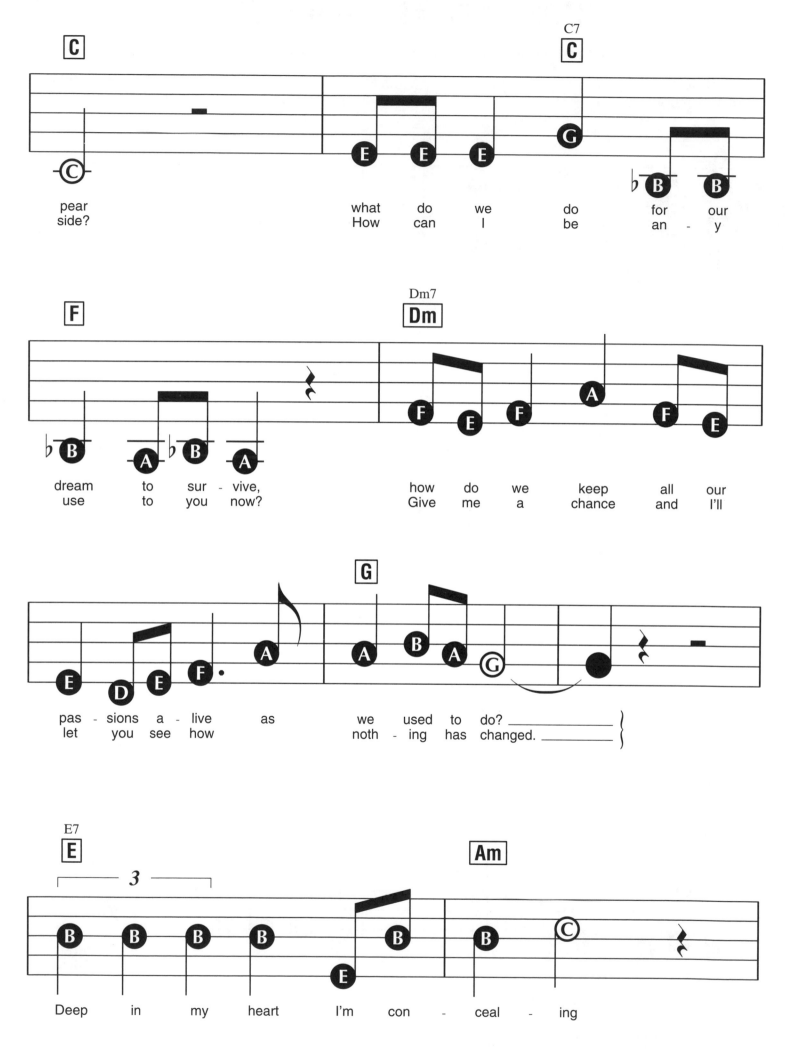

93

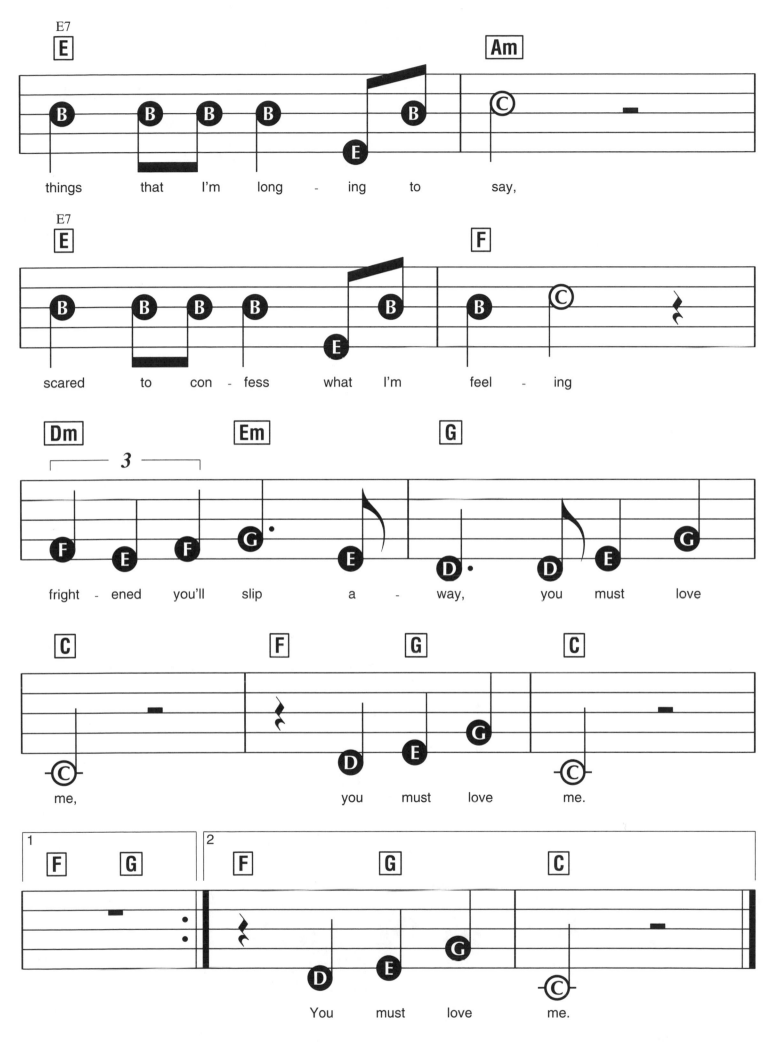

Young at Heart
from YOUNG AT HEART

Registration 1
Rhythm: Swing or Ballad

Words by Carolyn Leigh
Music by Johnny Richards

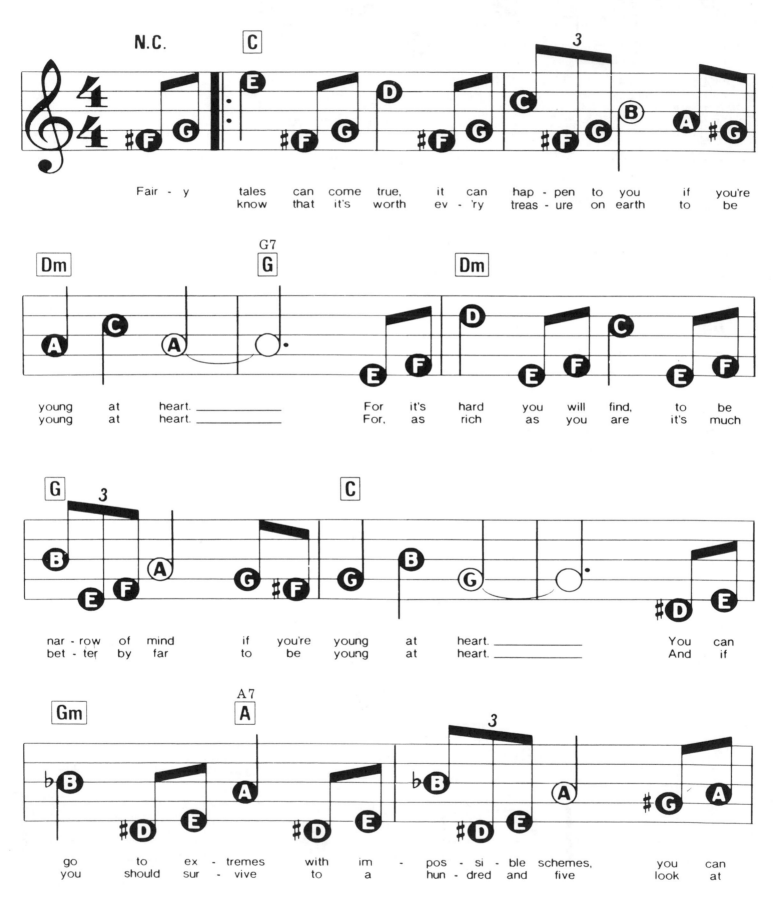

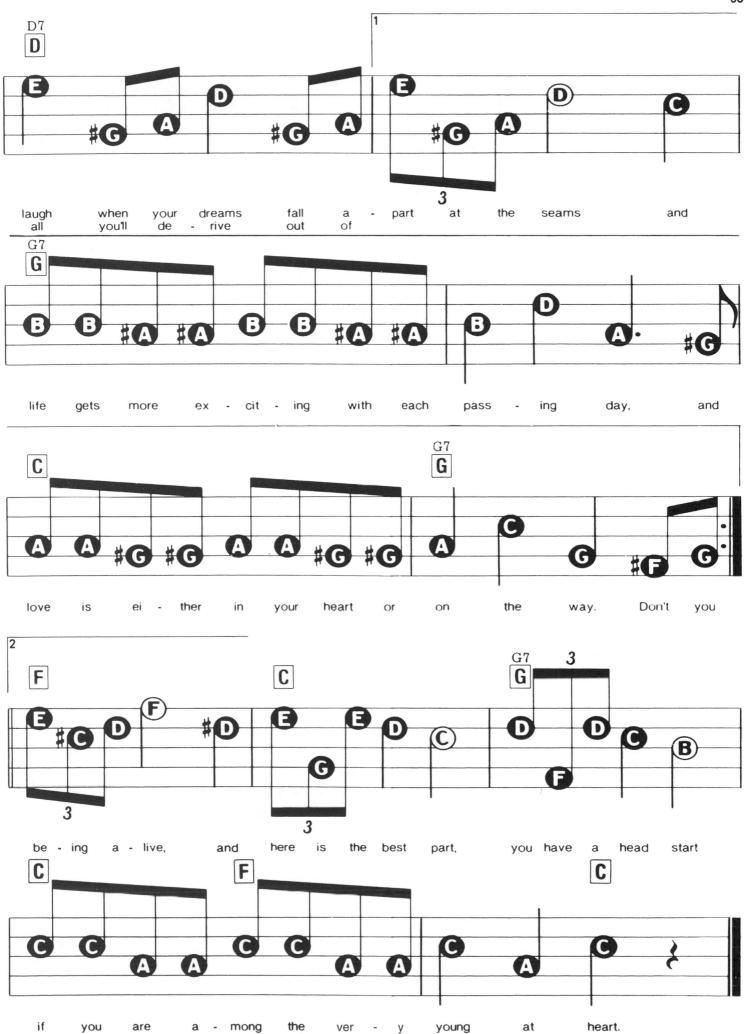

Registration Guide

- Match the Registration number on the song to the corresponding numbered category below. Select and activate an instrumental sound available on your instrument.

- Choose an automatic rhythm appropriate to the mood and style of the song. (Consult your Owner's Guide for proper operation of automatic rhythm features.)

- Adjust the tempo and volume controls to comfortable settings.

Registration

1	Mellow	Flutes, Clarinet, Oboe, Flugel Horn, Trombone, French Horn, Organ Flutes
2	Ensemble	Brass Section, Sax Section, Wind Ensemble, Full Organ, Theater Organ
3	Strings	Violin, Viola, Cello, Fiddle, String Ensemble, Pizzicato, Organ Strings
4	Guitars	Acoustic/Electric Guitars, Banjo, Mandolin, Dulcimer, Ukulele, Hawaiian Guitar
5	Mallets	Vibraphone, Marimba, Xylophone, Steel Drums, Bells, Celesta, Chimes
6	Liturgical	Pipe Organ, Hand Bells, Vocal Ensemble, Choir, Organ Flutes
7	Bright	Saxophones, Trumpet, Mute Trumpet, Synth Leads, Jazz/Gospel Organs
8	Piano	Piano, Electric Piano, Honky Tonk Piano, Harpsichord, Clavi
9	Novelty	Melodic Percussion, Wah Trumpet, Synth, Whistle, Kazoo, Perc. Organ
10	Bellows	Accordion, French Accordion, Mussette, Harmonica, Pump Organ, Bagpipes